TEST MATCH
SPECIAL 2

TEST MATCH
SPECIAL 2

Edited by
Peter Baxter

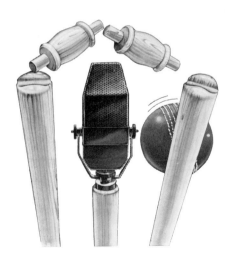

QUEEN ANNE PRESS
MACDONALD & CO (PUBLISHERS)
London & Sydney

A QUEEN ANNE PRESS BOOK

ACKNOWLEDGEMENTS
Designed by Pengilley Designs
Illustrations by Griffin

All photographs supplied by Peter Baxter
except the following:
BBC Hulton Picture Library; pages 20 and
23
BBC Publicity; pages 32 (top), 34 (top) and
171
BBC Stills Library; pages 7 and 100 (right)
Patrick Eagar; pages 78, 81, 82, 144 and 149
Bill Frindall; pages 68 and 130
Pauline Johnston; pages 26 to 39 (all
commentators except Fred Titmus), 154, 161
and 164
Rex Features; page 100 (left and centre)
Thames TV; page 90

Copyright © Queen Anne Press 1983
Scoresheets copyright © Bill Frindall

First published in Great Britain in 1983 by
Queen Anne Press
Macdonald & Co (Publishers) Ltd
London & Sydney

A BPCC plc Company

ISBN 0 356 09496 0

Filmset by Waterlow (Dunstable) Limited
A BPCC plc Company
Printed and bound in Great Britain by
The Alden Press, Oxford

CONTENTS

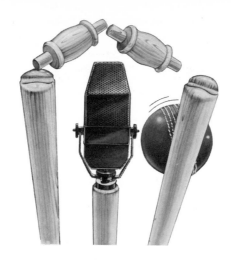

INTRODUCTION

Tim Rice

Although at the time of writing there is still one man in the England team older than me (and long may the selectors keep their faith in Bob Taylor) I have come to the grisly conclusion that I never going to play for my country at cricket. P. B. H. May was not present when I recently scored a career-best 39 v. Fernhurst, and I am beginning to wonder why I bothered to take 6 for 28 against Hit Or Miss when Big Alec never even apologised for his absence.

But I am not bitter – I have achieved the next best thing (some would say an even better thing). I have on more than one occasion become a part, albeit a brief and minor part, of the Test Match Special Team, a feat I have achieved in both England and Australia.

True, the dapper and perfectly formed producer Peter Baxter has not yet suggested tactfully to Christopher Martin-Jenkins that he should hang up his headphones to make way for me, and true, the time I squeezed into the commentary box at Headingley I was only there because it had been raining for days and even Brian Johnston was running out of one-liners. But I am still young enough to be able to live in hope for some years to come that I may one day get the permanent recognition from Baxter's selectorial team that May's has denied me.

But perhaps I am again being rather optimistic. To be chosen for the commentary box is an honour that only the highest skills can justify and is in its way a goal as far beyond the reach of ordinary mortals as is a place in the England XI. I am therefore particularly envious of those who have done both with ease – viz. T. E. Bailey, F. S. Trueman and A. R. Lewis.

It is quite extraordinary that whenever I have appeared on Radio 3 during a Test Match, almost everyone I know hears me. This never happens

when I am broadcasting elsewhere, attempting to sparkle for my living on other wavelengths. Next time I am desperately plugging some theatrical enterprise I shall somehow worm my way back into the TMS box. I am fed up with giving my all on arts programmes and confusing panel games to nil response from my nearest and dearest. If only one could get records played between overs – a number one hit would be certain.

During the final Test of the 1982/83 series in Australia, the Test Match Special team were forced to mix with ordinary mortals and commentate from seats high up in Sydney Cricket Ground's M. A. Noble stand. Consequently groupies like myself were actually able to sit next to their heroes as they unfolded the not always happy story to their countrymen back home in bed. There I discovered how simple cricket commentary isn't!

One of the features of an Australian series is that Henry Blofeld is permanently connected by yards of cable to three-quarters of Australia's radio stations from the moment he sets foot in the country. One of these stations was kind enough to show a glimmer of interest in my presence at the match and I was soldered into Henry's network where I proceeded to enthral farmers and the odd wombat in the outback with 'Evita' reminiscences. While I was speaking, a vital English wicket fell and I made the mistake of attempting to commentate on the dismissal and then of summarising the situation with Trevor Bailey-type incisiveness. I could almost hear my audience switching off, as I proceeded to make this crucial moment sound boring – in stark contrast to the gentlemen who have compiled this book, who are all capable of making boring incidents fascinating. That is why they appeal even to non-cricket lovers.

So I had better stick to being a listener, which is no hardship.

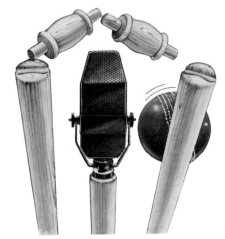

PLAIN TALES OF TMS

FRED TRUEMAN

Wherever cricketers gather, sooner or later, one of them will come up with a brain teaser. The question will be asked, 'Who did that?' or 'When and how did so-and-so happen?' It is no different in our commentary box. The TMS team are always trying to find questions to outdo fellow commentators. Bill Frindall usually has his book of answers beside him to nip in quickly, but my best one ever even had him flummoxed.

Everyone in the box tries to beat Brian Johnston with one of these questions and during the 1981 season he'd been throwing plenty of them at me. During the Saturday of the Lord's Test I suddenly remembered something I'd read in a cricket book in Yorkshire once. I put the question to Brian on the air.

'Can you tell me the Yorkshire cricketer who rode the Grand National winner?' We had the inevitable suspicious question from Bill asking if it meant that he had just sat on it, or ridden it round the garden. 'No,' I said, 'he was actually the winning jockey in the Grand National.' I have never seen Brian so well and truly stumped before. After a little while he gave up and asked me to tell him the answer. 'No,' I said, 'I'll give it to you on Monday morning.'

Never in my wildest dreams did I think that one cricket question would create so much interest. On the Sunday rest day I was playing in a charity match in Kent and people were coming up to me all the time asking the answer to the question. But I held out. 'You'll have to wait till Monday morning,' I told them. Several of them complained that they probably would not be able to listen at the right time or might miss it. I stayed silent.

Arriving at Lord's on Monday morning I must have been approached by twenty or thirty people asking what time I would be giving the answer. Up in the commentary box Peter Baxter, our producer, kept up the suspense by leaving me off until 12 o'clock, when Brian Johnston was due on. In the meantime the BBC switchboard had been jammed with callers who thought they knew the answer.

At 12 o'clock I took the summariser's chair alongside Brian, ready to deliver the answer. But B. J. was triumphant. 'Oh, Fred, I've got the answer to that question,' he said, almost casually. I couldn't believe it. 'But,' he went on, 'I have to be fair. I was rung up over the weekend by the chap's grandson.' So all was revealed. It was a man by the name of Wilson who played cricket with Yorkshire for a couple of seasons who actually did ride the Grand National winner in 1925. But Brian was able to go one better.

'Do you realise,' he said, 'he also won the V.C. in the First World War? He shot a Zeppelin down.' The great man had, as usual, had the last word. And I have been trying to find another question to stump him ever since!

CHRISTOPHER MARTIN-JENKINS

I am assured, not just by my parents but also by various aunts and schoolmasters, that from an early age I replied to the boring question adults often resort to when stuck for something to say to a child: 'I want to be a cricket commentator.' Now that, by a bit of work and a great deal of luck, I have achieved the ambition, I find myself still being asked a variation on the original inquiry. It is: 'what will you do next?' The fact is I do not particularly want to do anything next. Certainly not whilst there are Tests on which to commentate.

I am also frequently asked – I dare say we all are – if we really have so much fun on the programme as we sound as though we do. The answer is that there is no pretence whatsoever. It is, as far as I am concerned, the most enjoyable of all the many pleasant things I do under the label of 'work'. Cliche it may be, but to be paid for something you would, at least, if there were no mouths to feed, cheerfully do for nothing, is a great piece of good luck. Of course, as in any job, there are times when even commentary can seem like hard work. It is not necessarily when only one leg-bye is scored in twenty minutes. Indeed, apart from more than once being lucky enough to be on the air when England have won the Ashes, and also being there to describe a Mike Procter hat-trick (one of his many) and David Hookes's extraordinary burst of five successive fours amidst the tension of the Centenary Test in Melbourne, some of the most thrilling periods of commentary I have experienced have been those when nothing has been happening in the way of wickets and runs, but when one of cricket's classic 'any result is possible' situations has been slowly building up. I know I tend to be too romantic and to see excitement around the corner when others have written off a game as a sterile draw. The Test at Headingley in 1981, however, was a perfect example of why it is unwise to be too dogmatic about anything in cricket. The only time I can ever remember getting really irritated with my fellow commentators was when some of them gave up the match at the Oval in 1979 when India were chasing 438 to win the final Test. No hope, almost everyone said, forgetting the benignity of Harry Brind's pitch and the fact that India had already scored over 400 to win a Test. In the end I suppose I was wrong because they fell nine runs short. But what a game! It was one of many occasions, too, when a knowledge of cricket history has been vital to the job. If that is really the only time one has been irritated with one's team-mates it suggests a very remarkable team spirit. And that, coupled with the absolutely natural feel about the programme, is the secret of any success we have been lucky enough to have. A group of very different individuals we may be, but we work with, and for, each other in the happiest of atmospheres.

We are all very aware of our good fortune in being a part of Test Match Special and in no way complacent about it, knowing that we are commentating on Test cricket for the benefit of the listeners, not our own self-indulgence.

Happily, though, in our case, service and self-indulgence are one and the same!

PETER BAXTER

The laws of cricket take up thirty pages of *Wisden*. Each season they are added to by the Test and County Cricket Board's playing conditions for first-class matches. Now you would think that with all that legislation the most important item of all would be covered in a manner to dispel any doubts. I refer to the time for tea. A scorecard will tell you that tea is, perhaps, at 4.15 p.m. There is not enough room to go into the intricacies of what happens when nine wickets are down at 4.15 or when an innings ends at 3.50. Fortunately in Test Match Special we have our own resident expert on these matters – Brian Johnston.

In 1982 a new element was introduced into the timings of Test Matches with the adoption of the requirement for 96 overs to be bowled in a day. An adjunct to this admirable scheme was that tea could not be taken until only 35 overs remained. The time had to come when this latest regulation was sorely tested. It happened at Edgbaston.

They were running late with their overs when the ninth wicket fell at about four o'clock. Normally they would play on until the last wicket fell, or have tea after half an hour, but the number of overs should, we felt, come into it somewhere. Luckily Brian Johnston – the renowned expert on the subject – was at the microphone. Several copies of the playing conditions were scanned, but the answer was not obvious. Discussion was joined on the air – and off it – in the back of the box. I had my theory. Others had theirs, and Brian was the recipient of several divergent opinions whispered into his ear as he speculated.

Eventually I decided the listeners should be put out of their misery and the voice of authority should be consulted. At Edgbaston our commentary box in the pavilion is situated very close to the public address hut which is the domain of Lyn Clugsden, whose voice is well known to followers of Warwickshire. I had no doubt that he would have the answer. Up the few stairs I ran and out onto the roof where the hut stands. On opening the door I saw Lyn hunched over his desk. 'Ssh!' he waved me to keep quiet. I became aware that he was listening to Test Match Special.

'I just wanted to know,' I half whispered, 'what time the tea interval is going to be.'

'Ssh!' he said again. 'They're just discussing it on the radio – wait a minute and they'll have the answer.'

So I went back to the box and just guessed!

HENRY BLOFELD

It is, I am sure, the obvious friendliness and humour which distinguishes Test Match Special not only from commentaries on all other sports, but also from all the other Test Match commentary teams round the world. It is this which makes it such fun to be a part and, one hopes, such fun to listen to.

For Bob Willis's tour of Australia the BBC decided to mount its own commentary operation for the Test Matches, and so TMS went to Australia for the second time. In 1979-80 we had commentated on the three Tests between Australia and the West Indies although taking the ABC commentary for the England v Australia Tests.

TMS was able to field a pretty strong team throughout the tour, but it was different for each match with some members of the team coming out to Australia for two matches, some for three, and Brian Johnston for one at the end. Fred Trueman and I were the only two to take part in all the Tests.

We also utilised the services of one or two locals. Peter Loader, the enormously cheerful Surrey and England fast bowler who now lives in Perth, joined us as a comments man for the First Test at the WACA ground.

He always arrived at the commentary point in the morning bright eyed and indecently cheerful and made a point of asking those of us who were not feeling quite so well, what we had been up to the night before. It was simply that his powers of recovery were greater than ours!

Paul Sheahan, that elegant Victorian stroke-maker and brilliant cover fieldsman, now a housemaster at Geelong Grammar School, helped us with his highly entertaining commentary in the thrilling Fourth Test Match in Melbourne.

It was good to see how quickly Peter and Paul, or Scrubs and Timbers, to give them their playing-day nicknames, caught on to the BBC approach which is rather lighter than the more austere Australian commentary.

One of the problems which often catches out newcomers to TMS is what sounds the relatively simple job of handing over to the next commentator at the end of his twenty minute spell. When they have settled into their chairs and start rolling their tongues round memorable phrases, the awareness of time often completely disappears.

Paul enormously enjoys doing commentary. In Melbourne we were sitting on an open bench high up in the pavilion almost behind the bowler's arm. It was a little bit cramped and climbing in and out of our seats was a problem if one was to be in position for the first ball of the next over.

It is essential to accomplish this task without kicking Bill Frindall, nudging him to produce a splodge in his immaculate score sheets, knocking one of his books over or, worst of all, to spill a drink over one of these score sheets. If you do that he is unlikely to talk to you again until the next Ashes series but one!

Quite early in the match I was due to take over from Paul and positioned myself on the bench in front of the commentators. But Paul was relishing this particular spell even more than usual and cheerfully erudite phrases were tripping out of his mouth.

From time to time I looked round at him trying to catch his eye. When he had run over for fifteen minutes I said to Peter Baxter that Paul had better go on as it would be silly for me to take over just for five minutes.

I then went down to the press box to do some telephoned broadcasts to stations round Australia. When I returned to the BBC point, Paul, I hope, blushed slightly and we had a good laugh about it. I was sure that from then on he would at least get his timing right.

Not a bit of it! Each time from now until the end of the match I had almost literally to prise him out of his seat and he always pinched at least five minutes from me, but now he was doing it on purpose.

It became a joke which we discussed on the air although I am not sure what listeners twelve thousand miles away will have made of it in the early morning I told Paul once that if he had been as difficult to get out when he was a player, Australia would have won a few more Test Matches!

Paul and his delightful wife, Jane, have, for a long time, played an important part in every Melbourne Test Match. Jane always brings a marvellous picnic lunch consisting of the most delicious freshly cut sandwiches – she always says they are out of the deep freeze – and flagons of lovely cold white wine.

Those of us lucky enough to be asked, sundry journalists, broadcasters, friends of the family and, of course, the Sheahans two sweet young daughters, spread ourselves out in the sun in one of the enclosures in front of the press box, and prepare for a memorable interlude.

In the commentary box, Paul joined in the fun and the banter every bit as much as Peter Loader in Perth, and I am sure that they both must have provided a welcome change for English listeners who are so used to the usual TMS voices.

I shall never forget that Fourth Test, not least because I was lucky enough to be on the air when, just as Allan Border and Jeff Thomson seemed to have won the match for Australia, Thomson suddenly snicked Ian Botham. Chris Tavaré dropped the catch at second slip but Geoff Miller swooping round from first slip held on to the rebound and England had won by three runs. What a match it was!

TONY LEWIS

Wednesday 17th February 1982; another ball-by-ball commentary team was gathering. Henry Blofeld flew in from Australia: I flew out from London: Don Mosey, with producer Peter Baxter had been on the road all winter. This was the last match of England's long winter tour of India. The occasion, however, was unprecedented, even historic, if cricket history pleases you, because the venue was Colombo; the first official Test match ever played by Sri Lanka and the first chance for a Test Match Special team to be on the spot to describe the inauguration of a new test playing nation.

At the P. Sara Stadium the press and commentary building was not finished. The ascent would have had John Arlott turning for home without seeing a ball bowled. A ladder, lashed to concrete spines of the edifice and to various projecting wires actually sloped backwards, or so it felt. Climbing up carrying a weighty typewriter and a briefcase gave gravity an unfair advantage. After many repetitions of this one's arms felt inches longer.

The radio commentating table was neatly slotted in to the front of this upper deck. No walls or windows were complete. It was an al fresco exercise; delightful in the Sri Lankan sun, you might say. Unfortunately the self same rip-roaring sun, by close of play would be scalding the skin from every exposed piece of flesh on the left side of the body.

However, for me, nothing could spoil this celebration day. In the Seventies, I had led two MCC sides to Ceylon, as it then was called, to help them through their apprenticeship period. A minor tour in 1970 included such players as Geoff Boycott, Allan Jones, Keith Fletcher, John Hampshire, Bob Taylor, Geoff Arnold, Pat Pocock, Don Wilson, Don Shepherd. I shall never forget the roar at the Colombo Oval as Geoff Boycott had his stumps shattered by the second ball of the innings – G. Boycott b Kehelagamuwa 0. Coconuts fell off the trees up in Kandy; the dim light bulbs in the Nuwara-Eliya Golf Club, 8,000 feet up in the shadow of the Mount Pedro, peaked with the shock transmitted upwards through the tea plantations.

In 1973 it was the full England side, playing against such competitive but sporting folk, as Michael Tissera, Neil Chanmugan, Anura Tennakoon. England players were out in the colleges early in the mornings, making informal talks at assemblies, carrying on the encouragement for schoolboys at the nets after prayers. So, now in 1982, as commentary time came close, these were my personal memories, gilded by an affection for the country and those who have worked so hard at their cricket.

It was time for a new era of history. Don Mosey cleared his throat and had a couple of 'nets' at the pronounciation of the P. Saravanamuttu Stadium; Bob Willis turned at the end of his long run down below the commentary box, raced in and bowled to Bandula Warnapura, the Sri Lankan skipper. I must confess I felt the shiver of the occasion, of the privilege to have been there to describe it to British listeners so far away.

BILL FRINDALL

My commitment to Test match broadcasts became total in 1953 when Australia began their second post-war defence of the Ashes in England. I had been exiled in Canada during Bradman's successful expedition five years earlier, but Hassett's tour coincided with my third summer at Reigate Grammar School. On the first day of that historic series I had inveigled my way into the caretaker's cottage sited at the side of the main playground. Inside was a kindly cricket enthusiast and his television. Outside I had placed a blackboard to relay the score and details to the rest of the school at the end of each over. It was a much appreciated service; there was no continuous commentary on radio until 1957 and the transistor had not overwhelmed us. I can still hear the roars of delight which echoed round that scoreboard when Graeme Hole, a makeshift opener, was yorked by Alec Bedser's late inswing.

'Frindall's Test Match Score Service' continued for four school summers before giving way to sixth form studies and the arrival of ball-by-ball coverage on the wireless. I was already a devoted disciple of Arlott and Alston – much to my mother's irritation. She hated cricket and had to endure hours of commentary. Since I became one of the 'tormentors' she has hardly missed a ball!

After toying with architecture and publishing, I was conscripted for national service in the RAF. Unwittingly, I was preparing for my present work; a grounding in draftsmanship, an insight into book manufacture, and then full RAF courses in statistics and accountancy – they even simulated my TMS role by sending me monthly into a NATO bunker beneath Fontainebleau Forest to chart hits and missiles of mock WW3s.

The end of a short service commission coincided with the sudden death of my famous predecessor, Arthur Wrigley. That announcement prompted a daring letter to the Head of Outside Broadcasts, Charles Max-Muller, and resulted in an interview which eventually led to my introduction to the TMS team at Old Trafford, Manchester, on 2 June 1966. John Arlott, Robert Hudson and Roy Lawrence (Jamaica) were the commentators, while summaries were given by Norman Yardley, Freddie Brown and Jim Swanton. John had eased my debut with an early morning visit to Gibbs bookshop where I had purchased a complete set of 'Scores and Biographies' before heaving my several holdalls of books up two flights of stairs into a box that remains uniquely unchanged and inadequate today. Brian Johnston (then with television) slipped a Test Match Broadcasters' Club tie round my neck ('That will be £1 please!'), Conrad Hunte struck the very first ball from Jeff Jones to the cover-point boundary, Colin Milburn – on his debut, too – committed suicide twice (0 and 94) and an unrelated Gibbs completed an innings victory for West Indies in three days.

Now eighteen seasons and five tours of Australia on, I relive the fresh excitement of that nerve-racking first morning at the start of every Test – once I have breached the ground's security defences and done my impersonation of a porter off the Orient Express with my library. At least ninety minutes before we go on the air I will have unpacked books, files, stop watches, binoculars, pens, ruler, scoring sheets and frames, coffee flask and cushion. As I watch the ground filling up and greet Peter Baxter – usually the next arrival – I often wonder who is looking after that chalked scoreboard at Reigate!

TREVOR BAILEY

Although it has been said that Yorkshiremen do not like Southerners, my own experience has been exactly the reverse. As a player, I was probably better received in Yorkshire than anywhere else. The hospitality over the years which has been extended to me by the Yorkshire County Cricket Club has been magnificent, and my wife and I have more good friends in Yorkshire than anywhere else in the world, apart from our home town, where we were both born and have always lived. It follows, therefore, that I have a very special affection for the Headingley Tests which are also great annual reunions.

Headingley was also the scene of one of my worst moments in front of the microphone. In 1974, England met Pakistan in one of those special matches in which wickets are always falling and fortune for ever changing. Having broadcast for the first hour I went up, about one o'clock, to see my friends on the Yorkshire Committee. Normally this would have taken the form of a drink and a chat, but on this occasion the cricket was so fascinating that I went out on to the balcony watching the game. I had become so completely absorbed that I completely forgot the time, and also that I was due to do a four minute summary of the morning's play at 1.30. At about 1.28 I remembered! To understand my predicament it is necessary to know the geography of the Headingley ground. I suppose the actual distance between the Committee Room in the old pavilion and the commentary box is about a hundred yards, but this does not take into account the stairs. So I had to dash down at exactly the time when the other people were coming up for lunch, and then rush up the back of the Leeds Rugby Football Stand, also against a surging tide of spectators, to reach the commentary box. I arrived to sit down in front of the 'mike' and to hear the commentator say; 'And here to give you his thoughts on an absorbing morning's play is Trevor.'

I was certainly there. I certainly had plenty to talk about. But there was a snag. That hectic race against the clock had left me literally speechless. I wheezed out some largely unintelligible sounds before handing back with some difficulty to the studio and then collapsing with frustration. Within five minutes the phone calls started! One, not surprisingly from my wife, who feared I must have had a heart attack. But it taught me one valuable lesson – never try to broadcast if out of breath and unable to speak!

When I first joined Test Match Special (No, it simply could not have been all that long ago – it has been so much fun that time has stood still) Brian Johnston gave me some excellent advice. 'Always remember', he said, 'that you are talking to blind people. You have to provide the picture for them and remember they cannot see even the obvious.' We have since found that this is not always true, because there are a considerable number of people who watch the Tests on television, with the sound turned off, and the radio switched on. This was brought home to me when a lady telephoned to ask if the Australian fast bowler, Gilmour, was wearing a ring on his bowling hand, and whether or not this was fair. The question was relayed to me during the broadcast and I was able to confirm the ring, and although I did not think it would worry any batsman, wearing rings on the field is asking for trouble. A blow on the adorned finger can easily mean that the ring would have to be cut off – which can be both painful and expensive!

I have tried to remember Brian's advice, but sometimes forget, like the occasion when John Arlott asked me how to play the bouncer off the front foot. I instinctively rose from my chair behind the 'mike', thrust my left-foot firmly forward and fended off an imaginary bouncer, with left wrist facing, and in front of my eyes, coming back towards my head in order to drop the ball dead at my feet. I am sure that John understood the demonstration but it could hardly have been very illuminating for the listeners. Of all the commentators, I always thought that John Arlott painted the most vivid verbal pictures. I was lucky enough to be with him when he gave this classic description of the outstanding South African pace-bowler, Vincent Van der Bijl;

'Van der Bijl running up to bowl, looking like a much taller, stronger, younger and healthier version of Lord Longford'. This, very true, was followed by a slight pause, and then the punch-line delivered in that lovely unmistakable Hampshire accent – 'but not nearly so tolerant.'

Like most people who broadcast I have problems with the pronunciation of some words and names. One of the most troublesome was unquestionably Srinivasaraghavan Venkataraghavan. Brian Johnson's interpretation was 'Rent-a-Waggon.' I stuck simply to 'Venkat'.

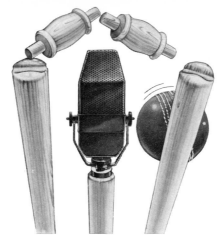

THE HISTORY OF TEST MATCH SPECIAL

John Arlott

Like Test cricket, cricket commentary began in Australia. In November 1922, before there was any regular broadcasting in Australia, a certain Lionel Watt, not otherwise an historic figure, was sent to the Sydney Cricket Ground where two elevens of New South Wales cricketers were playing in a testimonial for Charles Bannerman, who, 45 years before, had scored the first Test century. In the words of A. G. Moyes, the historian of Australian cricket, 'Watt was given a microphone and told to go on talking' – so he became the first cricket commentator. Commentary was thus established in Australia long before it was employed in England.

Much of the technique and programme content of Australian broadcasting derived from American and British sources. In commentary on cricket and horse racing – the two abiding national passions – however, Australia were pioneers, creating their own methods which are retained in their distinctive style today. The BBC did not, in general, quickly perceive the immense potential of the medium it controlled. It put out the more obvious material – music, plays and talks, and religious services – and soon, too, discussions and interview programmes. Commentary came appreciably later; radio's great, unique creation, the radio feature, much later still.

Simply enough, as soon as broadcasting equipment became even remotely portable, 'the wireless' possessed the unique ability to disseminate news, at the moment it occurred, to a mass audience. That is commentary reduced to its simplest terms. Its value, and the extent of public hunger for it, were demonstrated by the coverage of the General Strike in 1926. Even then, commentary – certainly sporting commentary – hardly entered the minds of the broadcasting administrators as a practical undertaking. That occurred in the following year, spurred by three factors: the charter of 1927 gave the BBC the right to send its reporters to important events; Lance Sieveking, probably the outstanding and most creative pioneer of British broadcasting was given a fairly free hand in programme-making; on an exploratory visit to the United States, he heard some sporting – baseball – commentary, and came home determined to experiment with the idea.

The first commentator Sieveking engaged was Captain H. B. T. (Teddy) Wakelam, a wartime soldier, by then a construction engineer who had played rugby for the Harlequins. Sieveking had never met him but, on the recommendation of a friend who described him as a good talker about rugby, after a single meeting, a brief audition and a rather sketchy practice run, he was taken to Twickenham to broadcast the England-Wales rugby international. The producer's planning included – most perceptively – a formerly sighted blind man from St Dunstan's posted in front of the box as a guinea-pig listener; a 'number two', or 'Doctor Watson' – Charles Lapworth – to prompt with reasonable questions, live; and Sieveking himself beside the box to make suggestions off-mike.

The choice was fortunate. Wakelam was a natural talker with a reasonable vocabulary, a good rugby mind, and a conscious determination to avoid journalese. On this occasion, determined to satisfy his St Dunstan's man, he galloped away until he all but lost breath. He confessed indeed – mark of a natural commentator – that the material went in through the eyes, out through the mouth and that he subsequently recollected virtually nothing of what he had described. That was the first sporting commentary in British radio. Sieveking, whose opinion was decisive, was satisfied. Wakelam not only continued to broadcast rugby but, in the same year, made the first soccer broadcast (an Arsenal match at Highbury) and, soon afterwards, the first on lawn tennis (the Wimbledon Championships of 1927). He continued with tennis commentary until the second world war.

The first cricket commentary, too, took place in 1927: on 14 May – Essex v New Zealanders at Leyton. It was made by Plum – later Sir Pelham – Warner who, in his lifetime as player, manager, selector, reporter, historian, administrator and, eventually, the elder statesman, of the English game, watched, beyond all reasonable argument, more first-class cricket than anyone else who ever lived. Authoritative as he was, his voice was subdued, almost expressionless, and he made little impact. He was followed by the Rev F. H. Gillingham, a powerful batsman for Essex whose caricature in *Vanity Fair* was titled 'Cricketing Christianity'. Normally a good and forthright talker, he had the ill-luck to be announced for his first quarter-hour when rain had prevented even the start of play. He struggled on to fill his time out of nothing, but hardly pleased his masters when, ingeniously, but ingenuously, he proceeded to read out the advertisements on the hoardings round The Oval; such blatant publicity that the BBC shuddered to its corporate spine.

So Teddy Wakelam, who had played the game at good club level for many years, became the third cricket commentator. Lord's did not even admit broadcasting equipment to the ground and Wakelam, with Alan Howland as his number two, covered a Surrey-Middlesex match at The Oval. He was unlucky in that the early Surrey batting – potentially so splendidly entertaining – collapsed, and Andrew Sandham, skilfully, valuably, but unexcitingly, shored it up with a long slow innings. Wakelam laboured; as most professional broadcasters would have done in those days.

At this time Lance Sieveking moved on to the drama department and major innovations there. Gerald Cock, an alertly minded barrister, took over from him on outside broadcasts. Wakelam – justifiably recognised as the senior and most capable sporting commentator, but obviously most disappointed by his venture into cricket – convinced the new departmental head that the game was too dull to be good broadcasting material. 'That afternoon put paid to cricket as a real running commentary sport,' he wrote.

Interestingly – even sadly – Wakelam could still write, eleven years afterwards in his autobiography, *Half Time* (1938): 'When, once again, it [cricket] reappeared in the programme, in the capable hands of Howard Marshall, the method of putting it over had considerably changed and the present system of several eye-witness accounts, interspersed with very short, and very occasional, ball-by-ball commentaries, was inaugurated.'

While, no doubt, Wakelam did much for rugby, possibly soccer, and most certainly tennis, in the field of radio commentary, it must be wondered how much he set back cricket broadcasting. It seems certain that Cock accepted his sadly subjective view of it as definitive; and it may well, therefore, have coloured many subsequent planning decisions. Thus Howard Marshall, who had a most pleasing touch in commentary, was, as Wakelam accurately pointed out, given little opportunity for it in programme allocations.

There were some domestic broadcasts on the Australian series of 1930; but they did not amount to even one piece a day until the fifth Test, when there were some few minutes of commentary. Otherwise, only summaries were put out. They were done by M. K. Foster, of that famous cricketing family, and a captain of Worcestershire; Archie MacLaren, the old Lancashire and England captain; and, on the second, third and fifth Tests, Aubrey Faulkner, the former South African all-rounder, then running a highly successful cricket school in London. In the fifth – Oval – Test the BBC employed the identifying assistant, already established for rugby and soccer matches, whose duty was to place the centre of play for the listener in 'square two', 'square four', or wherever, corresponding with a plan published in the *Radio Times*. The method was adopted for the first, and last, time in cricket broadcasting at The Oval. The man responsible was John Snagge, who became an important broadcaster in several fields. The experiment was not a success in the way hoped for, but it did save a situation when Faulkner fell ill and John Snagge was left to soldier through alone.

Although commentary was now an accepted form of broadcasting, the BBC still showed no enthusiasm for cricket. It was effectively thrust upon the British listening public through the series played by Douglas Jardine's

Pioneers of cricket broadcasting: *Top left* Lance Sieveking, producer; *Top right* Sir Pelham Warner, the first commentator in 1927; *Above* Michael Standing.

England side of 1932-33 in Australia. In Australia a cricket commentary 'war' was already in progress, assisted by the fact of the vast distances. They had already resolved the issue of broadcasting affecting match attendances. Indeed, one of the first and most difficult problems of the newly formed Australian Broadcasting Commission in 1932 was to reconcile the intense competition between the private companies who competed so savagely for cricket listeners across its great distances. By historic chance, too, this was the most controversial of all Test rubbers – the Body-Line series. In Australia, players were whisked by car from ground to studio to broadcast their views on events available to the British public only later through the newspapers. Throughout Britain the special early editions of the evening papers, carrying reports on the play, constantly sold out to enthusiasts moved to immense interest by the fast bowling tactic employed to defeat the hitherto invulnerable Bradman. Yet, for the first Test, the BBC provided no more than summarised scores in the news bulletins.

By contrast, the French commercial stations broadcasting to Britain were quick to take the opportunity. Radio Paris put out two separate quarter-hour periods of detailed score with critical comment. Poste Parisien was more ambitious. It brought over Alan Fairfax, the New South Wales all-rounder who had been a member of the 1930 Australian team in England, and sat him in a studio in the Eiffel Tower. There he was fed highly detailed cables of virtually every event of play immediately after it took place. His background knowledge enabled him to put flesh on the hard facts, and his use of the present tense, and his strong Australian accent, imparted an air of authenticity. Indeed, it might well be argued that Alan Fairfax did more than anyone else to create a demand for cricket commentary in England. Moreover, his broadcasts, billed as 'At intervals from 6 a.m. Relay of the Test Match from Australia', went on almost unbroken, thus translating a day's play into two hours of highly concentrated 'synthetic' commentary. Certainly the motor firm which sponsored his broadcasts happily paid for the radio time – with advertisements, of course – directed at Britain before breakfast. Certainly, too, anyone with an interest in cricket who had access to a radio set in that winter of 1932-33 will still remember the Fairfax broadcasts as both compelling and novel. This type of composed commentary was employed by the Australians as late as the 1938 tour of England when the companies there feared they could not rely on the live service from England so set up their own cable offices on the ground.

After the first Test, the BBC characteristically exploited its highly developed technical resources, and devotion to authenticity, by using the old 'Empire' short wave service to broadcast direct from the ground a ten-minute eye witness account by Alan Kippax who, dropped from the Australian team after the first Test of the rubber, watched the remainder as a reporter.

As the series progressed, increasingly dramatically, controversially and, most important in this country, with a series of wins for Jardine's team, a demand was created in Britain for coverage of Test cricket which could not be gainsaid. By happy historic coincidence, too, when the Australians paid their next visit – in 1934 – the BBC had discovered a highly suitable and successful cricket broadcaster. Howard Marshall was an Oxford rugby blue; he had played cricket to 'Authentic' standard and reported it for the now defunct *Westminster Gazette* until it ceased publication in 1927 when he joined the BBC. Beginning as an announcer and newsreader, he covered rugby matches and current events – such as the gathering of the hunger marchers in Hyde Park – and became a radio professional, developing that lack of fear of – and familiarity with – the microphone which is an essential for the successful ad lib broadcaster.

Marshall was eminently suited to cricket: he had a deep, warm, unhurried voice; a respect for the hard news of event, and a friendly feeling towards the men who played the game. Unhappily for him, some factors still militated against wholehearted commitment to cricket commentary in England. The first was the attitude of the cricketing establishment. MCC, for instance, still would not allow a broadcast to take place from within Lord's. Marshall had to watch the Test Match from his allotted seat in the press box and then, each interval, make his way to a nearby point to broadcast.

Much of Howard Marshall's most impressive work was, in effect, reconstituted. He was a reflective broadcaster and therein lay his strength. When, however, he was given the chance of commentary in 1938, and later in wartime matches, he tended, from sheer lack of experience, to be crucial seconds behind the play. So, as he described a bowler coming in to bowl, the microphone caught the sound of the applause for the boundary struck from him. He probably is most richly remembered for his vivid account of Hedley Verity's match at Lord's in 1934 when, with seven for 61 and eight for 43, that Yorkshire slow left-arm bowler gave England their only win in a series dominated by Bradman, and given its decisive twist by the spin of Grimmett and O'Reilly.

Up to the outbreak of the second world war, Marshall often worked in double harness with Michael Standing, a staff member of the BBC, a good club cricketer with an alert mind and a good turn of phrase. They were at times reinforced by E. W. (Jim) Swanton of *The Daily Telegraph* who had broadcast the 1938-39 English tour in South Africa, where in his first Test he had the commentator's gift of a hat trick – by Tom Goddard of Gloucestershire – on the old Wanderers ground at Johannesburg.

By the time post-war cricket began, Marshall had gone into industry; and Standing had taken a senior executive post in the Corporation.

Once more cricket broadcasting was given a fillip by historic circumstances. For a vast number of English people the resumption of the first-class game was a nostalgic – indeed, euphoric – symbol of the post-war return to normality. That feeling was emphasised by England's Test win over India in 1946; even more by the golden 1947 summer of Compton and Edrich, with the defeat of South Africa; and finally – and finally probably is the right word – by the visit of Bradman's Australians in 1948.

C. B. Fry, the 'comments' man, and John Arlott in action in 1949.

The new post-war head of Outside Broadcasts was S. J. de Lotbinière (Lobby) who contributed more to the development of commentary than any other holder of that office. He had an analytical mind; and his insistence on the 'pyramid' – the shaping of information from the peak outwards and downwards to fit the time available – remains the ideal structure for commentary or summary. Although – or, perhaps, indeed, because – he had little personal interest in cricket (or any other sport), he was a most perceptive critic of style or content, able to put his finger precisely on flaws, faults or wrong tendencies. Without hurry, and never too far ahead of public or – by no means always identical – official BBC opinion, he shrewdly extended commentary, especially in the field of cricket. His first task was to build a commentary team to replace Marshall and Standing.

In the 1946 Indian series the domestic audience was given little more than two hours a day of commentary and summary, all on the Light Programme, plus a close of play score in news bulletins. The main team consisted of Rex Alston and E. W. Swanton, with Arthur Gilligan, the amiable former captain of Sussex and England, and the erudite, idiosyncratic and admirably fluent C. B. Fry helping out, largely with comments. Rex Alston, Cambridge running blue, cricketer for Bedfordshire and sometime school-master who had joined the BBC in 1942 as a newsreader and announcer, had become an Outside Broadcasts assistant with responsibility for cricket, rugby and athletics. Jim Swanton carried on from pre-war days; he subsequently switched to television commentary and then – probably most effectively – to admirably authoritative summaries on both sound and vision. For Indian listeners, J. Arlott, a literary programmes producer in the Eastern Service, broadcast short commentary-cum-summary periods in English; Abdul Hamid Sheikh, a newsreader in the same department, in Hindi.

For the 1947 South African tour series, Messrs Alston and Swanton were joined again by C. B. Fry and Arthur Gilligan. Gilligan already had some years' experience as an opinions man on Australian radio, where 'What do you think, Arthur?' – which invariably heralded the mildest of comments – became a national gag. I was doing commentary to South Africa and, increasingly, on the domestic air, travelling with the touring side, as did Dana Niehaus, a senior sports reporter for an Afrikaans newspaper who gave summaries in that language.

The series against Bradman's 1948 Australians was a resounding success in every way except in terms of match results, for England. Even that fact could not blunt the immense public hunger for cricket reflected in huge crowds, not only at the Tests but at the tourists' fixtures with the counties, and in the radio listening figures. It was estimated that the number of sound-radio listeners for the last day of the fourth – Headingley – Test, when England half promised to win, was as high as seven million. It is doubtful if cricket commentary has ever attracted a larger audience. Sound radio had that story to itself for, although television of cricket had begun in 1938, its coverage was confined to the two London Tests until 1950 (Nottingham) and 1952 (Manchester and Leeds).

The sound-radio team was Rex Alston, E. W. Swanton, Alan McGilvray – the Australian commentator who had succeeded Don Bradman as pre-war captain of New South Wales – and myself; with comments and opinions from Arthur Gilligan, C. B. Fry, Herbert Sutcliffe and George Duckworth. It is worth noting that, even as late as this, the Australian Broadcasting Commission sent a senior representative to maintain a running service of cables in case reception of the short-wave broadcast was unsatisfactory, when they could provide synthetic commentary of the 1932 Fairfax type. That did not prove necessary. BBC's short-wave transmission proved satisfactory.

The immense enthusiasm led to a substantial growth in cricket broadcasting, especially of the basic county game, so essential for understanding and full appreciation of the play at Test level. Confirmed by the substantial attendances at county matches, the Regions – London, West, Midlands and North – began to opt out of basic Home Service programmes to cover 'their' Championship cricket. Some five hours a match afforded a sound training and experience for the commentators fortunate enough to be working at that time. By then several others had put their names on their chairbacks. They included Peter Cranmer – rugby international and captain of Warwickshire – Alan Gibson, Robert Hudson, and Peter West.

That pattern continued until 1969 after which it became one of the casualties of 'Broadcasting in the Seventies'. Meanwhile, Test coverage had grown steadily from the two hours of 1946, but there proved to be a number of obstacles such as fixed programmes – especially news bulletins – to daylong commentary. The term 'Test Match Special' was already in use before that complete coverage was first achieved (under the production of Michael Tuke-Hastings in 1957) by dint of switching between Light, Home and Third programmes.

From the rejection of cricket as programme material in 1927; and as subject for sustained commentary until 1938, the progress of Test Match Special is an unexpected story of prosperity. It has come to be accepted primarily, one hopes, for the instant service it provides of events in the match in progress. It has, though, appealed to many listeners relatively unconcerned with the course of play. Immense interest obviously has been generated by the casual chat which goes on when rain stops play and is often – in this writer's humble opinion, unpardonably – quite unconnected with cricket and irrelevant to the situation. It is an unusual formula for radio: a medley of views and ideas expressed by, often, as many as six voices – though the number and its members vary constantly as one leaves and another comes in – with no planned theme or direction, but spun at random as one idea prompts another. It is true that those taking part are all professional talkers but even that does not fully account for the apparent listener appeal of the output. It probably is an amalgam of several factors. It is, of course, extemely English, which is not a chauvinistic comment. It seems to have a considerable nostalgic impact on expatriate English people, especially in Australia – before they are conditioned to the methods there – and New Zealand. The relatively slow turnover of broadcasters means that they know one another well, can prod reactions with reasonable certainty. There is, too, especially since Peter Baxter took over as producer, an extremely friendly atmosphere in the box. To have observed only four instances of sharpness in the space of thirty-five years argues a considerable communal good humour. There has, too, always been so much leg-pulling that pomposity is impossible.

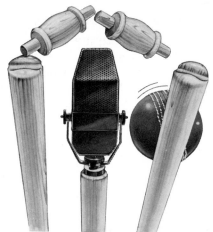

THE 1983 COMMENTATORS
─── Christopher Martin-Jenkins ───

THE REGULARS

CHRISTOPHER MARTIN-JENKINS.
It is probably indicative of Christopher's talents that after his departure from the staff post of BBC Cricket Correspondent at the end of 1980, there was a void in that job. Happily, his appointment as editor of *The Cricketer* enables him to operate as a freelance commentator.

Born on 20 January 1945, CMJ, as he is known to everyone in broadcasting (and quite a few listeners) is a more than useful club cricketer who is always determined to keep precious days set aside to play the game which gives us all our living. He is a benevolent father of three, living deep in the Sussex countryside with his utterly unflappable wife, Judy.

In the game he is popular and respected – charitable critic and technically a fine commentator. Terry Wogan has referred often to 'a short report by a very tall broadcaster' – six foot three he is, and short reports were certainly his original great strength. For years as the BBC's man on tour his were the reports everyone woke up to hear. His reporting technique remains a model for us all. **P.B.**

> So here are Christopher's pen pictures of his colleagues of the commentary box in 1983 when, thanks to the Prudential World Cup, there were rather more than usual.

BRIAN JOHNSTON. *Born 24 June, 1912.*
Irrepressible, that's what you are. This variation on the old lyrics made famous by Nat King Cole might serve as the theme song for one of the best loved voices, and best loved personalities, in radio. Like Cleopatra, 'age cannot wither him nor custom stale his infinite variety.'

'Infinite variety' may, actually, be stretching a point, although there is almost no statement that B.J. cannot turn into a pun, and no situation, cricketing or otherwise, in which he cannot find some humour.

To criticise Brian, as some have recently done, for excessive levity, or frivolity, is, in my view, quite unfair. If all the fun and light-heartedness which he brings to his commentaries, greatly to the enjoyment of most of his listeners, were at the expense of telling the story of the game in progress, the criticism would be merited. But it is not. Listeners can rely on a fair and accurate description of the match as well as an entertaining one.

No-one loves cricket more than Brian Johnston and few know the game better or do more to enhance its good name. Seventy-one in June, 1983, he seemed then about as likely to retire as Clive Lloyd. If he ever does, his marvellous sense of fun and peerless gift of the gab would be missed both by his colleagues in the box and his listeners.

HENRY BLOFELD. *Born 23 September, 1939.*
A deliberate eccentric, Henry Blofly, as the Australians affectionately call him, lives for cricket, pursuing it round the globe with only slightly less enthusiasm than he follows his ladies.

Possessed of more energy than Derek Randall and Mrs Thatcher put together (a formidable combination) he recently created a new United Australian and All Comers record (admittedly wind-assisted) by producing more girl-friends in one Test match than any other man, Bill Frindall included. The record was established during the Perth Test match of 1982/83 when on one day he came up with three different girls in three successive sessions of play on the second day. Each was introduced as 'Darling' to his fellow commentators and each was assured by his loyal colleagues that Henry had talked about no-one else but her since their meeting. The problem, however, was that each thought she was dining with him that night. He had to phone round to each to say that, unfortunately, his sports editor had demanded an unexpected story which could not wait.

Indeed the excuse might easily have been valid for, apart from his bubbling, helter-skelter commentaries, Henry works harder than anyone as cricket reporter for newspapers all round the world. He was once unwise enough to boast as much to Alan Gibson during an early season match in

The Parks at Oxford and Alan never let him forget it: for the rest of the season he quoted extensively from the cricketing correspondent of the 'Baltimore Globe', the 'Khallej Express', the 'Maryland Echo', the 'Prague Clarion' and other apocryphal newspapers.

To see Henry servicing the many Australian radio stations he works for during the English winter is to see the personification of perpetual motion. Moreover he speaks with authority, having been a gifted wicket-keeper-batsman himself (for Eton, Cambridge and Norfolk) and as one who watches the game all the year round.

His obsession with buses, trains and planes caused his producer to ban the mention of them a season or two back. Undaunted, Henry turned to helicopters and then excelled himself by revealing, exclusively, that a butterfly had just walked across the pitch at The Oval. You have to be very hawk-eyed to see butterflies walking!

DON MOSEY. *Born 3 October, 1924.*
Sharp-witted and, sometimes, razor tongued, Don Mosey has a soft heart a couple of chins below a face which can change from pink merriment to purple fury in a split second of indignation.

Some apparently innocent incident on the field, or a colleague's favourable comparison of, say, Ian Botham with Wilfred Rhodes, or Alan Davidson with George Hirst, may trigger a minor paroxism as sudden as an April shower.

But, as John of Gaunt observed, 'this rash fierce blaze of riot cannot last . . . Sudden storms are short.' The Alderman positively thrives on being irascible, or pretending to be. He also has a great sense of humour, deep knowledge of a wide range of subjects and a fine command of the language.

These are qualities which fit him admirably for the pleasurable task of commentating on cricket. Fiercely loyal to Yorkshire, though he lives across the Pennines on Morecambe Bay, Don loves travelling, especially to New Zealand where he returns for the BBC in 1984. His son, Ian, is an outstanding professional golfer, and his wife Jo, always referred to with rough affection as 'The Bride', is a teacher.

TONY LEWIS. *Born 6 July, 1938.*
Captain of England in his first Test, and victorious captain at that, Tony Lewis's only problem since retiring from cricket soon after leading England with great credit on the 1972/3 tour of India and Pakistan, has been to decide what work not to do. A naturally gifted writer and broadcaster, as indeed he was a batsman, he has been in demand by newspapers, radio and television though I suspect that radio is his favourite medium.

One would be tempted to call Tony a talented all-rounder if there were not a danger that this might tempt him to put himself forward as a serious bowler in the cricket he still plays for such teams as Old England, the Arabs and the Heartaches. He did actually once have figures of three for 18 for Glamorgan against Somerset but this was only the exception which proves every rule.

More to the point, he captained Glamorgan to their second Championship in 1969 and for Cambridge, Glamorgan and England, he hit, in all, 30 centuries. But for a knee injury he might well have hit more than his one Test hundred, scored at Kanpur. If I dwell on these achievements more than on the still greater successes enjoyed by Fred Trueman and Trevor Bailey, it is mainly because Tony is so modest about them.

F. S. TRUEMAN. *Born 6 February, 1931.*
It says something for the fame of any cricketer if when suffering from an illness he becomes the subject of a large headline in a newspaper in the Middle East. It happened that I was in Dubai in March 1983 when Fred went down with a virus soon after his return to England from Australia. The headline read: MYSTERY ILLNESS HITS ENGLAND CRICKETER

Most viruses are mysteries but few cricketers and certainly very few retired ones, command that sort of attention. Fred does so not simply because of the weight of his achievements as a cricketer – 307 Test wickets – but also because he was such a rich character, a showman on the field and a brilliant raconteur, actor, and deliberately boastful conversationalist off it. Fred always rises to an audience and always did. That is why he is such a natural broadcaster.

Mix his ready wit with his deep knowledge of the game, both technical and historical, and you will understand why he is so popular on Test Match Special. Sometimes as rambling and long-winded as Trevor Bailey is succinct, Fred is a sympathetic commentator to work with, opinionated, as any good Yorkshireman always is, but every bit as ready with praise as he is with criticisms and condemnations.

He is a great chap to have in the box when it is raining, telling any number of good cricket stories when we are on the air and one or two equally good unquotable ones if ever we hand back to the studio! He certainly proves the cliché 'Its the way you tell 'em that counts.' He makes the most ordinary story sound funny and, moreover, I have heard him tell the same tale twenty times and laughed as much on each occasion.

TREVOR BAILEY. *Born 3 December, 1923.*
In the field, and to a certain extent with a bat in his hands too, Trevor Bailey used to be confident, decisive and sharp. His commentaries in the box are just the same. Perhaps more so. If he could, Trevor would sum up an entire five day Test match during the course of its first five minutes – or even in the period as the captains walk back to the pavilion having made the toss! He is the greatest distiller since Johnnie Walker!

Nine times out of ten, a remarkably high proportion, he gets his predictions, or his assessments of a player or the state of the match, absolutely right. But because of his relish for the decisive utterance, his delight in putting his head on the block, he sometimes gets it comprehensively chopped off. Comfortably seated in the corner of the box, like a well fed judge secure in his knowledge of the law and of all criminals, he will make his first magisterial prediction five minutes after the start of the broadcast on the opening day of a Test match. 'Good pitch, sunny day, good toss to win, had to bat, moderate attack, one good bowler, Hadlee, the rest good county second seamers and one moderate spinner of Essex League standard, England at the end of the day . . . (slight dramatic pause) . . . 260 for three.'

If at the end of the first day England should happen to have been bowled out for 180, Hadlee taking only two wickets, the moderate seamers sharing five others and the no-hoper spinner picking up three for eight in eleven overs which Laker in his prime would have been pleased with, no-one would laugh more at the joke than Trevor. When you are usually right, you can afford to laugh when you are occasionally wrong.

In any case he enjoys a good joke about anything; enjoys life generally. A loyal husband and father he never misses any chance to go home to his house in 'The Drive', Westcliff. It ought, we have all decided, to be called 'The Forward Defensive.'

BILL FRINDALL. *Born 3 March, 1939.*
Sir Leonard Hutton, never very precise in the matter of nomenclature, once came into the commentary box during a Test match at The Oval and watched the match with half of one eye whilst reading the Financial Times with the other one and a half. After he had been with us half an hour or so, there was a flurry of activity on the field and an even greater one in the box, because someone had broken a record and Bill was suddenly twitching in his chair like a condemned man given too small a current. At the end of the over he got his chance to speak and delivered himself of a detailed discourse on the new record and its previous holders. Sir Leonard lowered his paper,

looked at me and said in a slightly conspiratorial whisper 'Is that Bill Frindly'?

None of the regular listeners to TMS would have been in any doubt, because Bill has deservedly made himself famous by his expertise as a scorer and statistician. The key to his success, apart from his sharp mind and intense capacity for hard and detailed work, is the fact that he is so painstaking about all he does. He is, in short, a perfectionist. Like John Arlott, Bill loves his fresh air and since John's retirement he is the first to open the window of the box as wide as possible on even the coldest days. Yet if there is the slightest suspicion of a drop of rain approaching, he will leap up like a frightened hen, shutting the window no matter how the noise of it may sound over the air, because a drop of rain on one of his immaculate scorecards would be to him like a discordant note to Tchaikovsky.

Most of the 'noises off' which you may hear if listening to TMS are the work of William Frindall. An inveterate snorter and sniggerer, he never misses a commentator's slip or unintended double entendre, and he is forever switching pencils and biros, or clicking stopwatches, or burrowing into heavy cricketing tomes. Because he is so well organised he always knows any records which may be likely to fall in any given day and the answer to the most obscure queston is seldom far from his fingertips.

He is almost always first to arrive, unless Peter Baxter beats him to it, and at lunch he is first to leave the box, eschewing any sponsor's packed lunch and instead making straight for a pre-arranged spot in the sun where a handmaiden will be awaiting him with a three course meal and a crisp white wine.

His job requires intense concentration and his commitment to the job is positively Boycottian.

Out of the box he leads exactly the life he wants to lead. That includes a good deal of playing cricket as a slightly eccentric, but nonetheless a useful fast bowler for a wide variety of clubs including his own – The Malta-maniacs.

JOINING US FOR THE PRUDENTIAL WORLD CUP

MICHAEL CAREY. *Born 5 January, 1936.* Primarily a journalist, who for a number of years worked mainly in cricket and football as a free-lance writer in the Midlands, Mike Carey is an accomplished and experienced sports writer who had some hard acts to follow when taking over in 1982 as cricket correspondent of the *Daily Telegraph*.

His debut for Test Match Special was made in the Ashes series in Australia in 1982/83 but he had already done a good deal of work for Radio Derby, on his home patch, and on television for both ITV and the BBC.

His greatest qualities are a sense of humour and a sharp wit. He was not a serious cricketer himself, but is fitter than a good many of his colleagues, having a liking for jogging.

NORMAN CUDDEFORD. *Born 8 January, 1933.*

A versatile performer, highly professional for one who has made broadcasting more a hobby than a profession, Norman's main employment is as a partner in a thriving Insurance Broking firm in the city. Without removing either his pin-stripe suit or his rolled umbrella, he can switch with unruffled calm to talking about athletics, tennis or cricket, all sports of which he has a wide knowledge. Only once has that calm been temporarily interrupted. Once called in on Radio 4 to give a latest score from a Test match commentary he was monitoring, he was asked: 'Norman can you bring us up to date with the details?' Thinking it was just a 'test run' and that he was not really on the air, Norman made the immortal reply. 'No I'm awfully sorry, I can't.'

RALPH DELLOR. *Born 19 January, 1948.*

'One of the newer fellas', as Crosby said of Sinatra in High Society, Ralph Dellor is already well known to listeners to Radio London, for whom he does Sunday commentaries, and also on The British Forces Network for whom he does a good deal of sports reporting and producing.

Light and pleasant of style, he is a versatile and concientious performer who also reports Soccer for, amongst others, Radio 2. He has contributed to a book on The Ashes and co-ordinates the production, advertising and distribution of the John Player League programme used on Sundays by the majority of the first-class counties.

MIKE DENNESS. *Born 1 December, 1940.*

A more relaxed character than he sometimes was in the high-pressure days of his England captaincy, Mike Denness can look back with great pride on his achievements on the cricket field. People call Douglas Jardine a Scot but in the sense of being born and bred there he was not a thorough Caledonian in the way Denness is: thus he is unique in being the only Scotsman to captain England and, except in Australia in 1974/75 when his problems were insoluable anyway against Lillee and Thomson at their peak, he was a successful captain, too. He led by example on the field and often played his best innings when the chips were down. His 188 in the Melbourne Test was a personal triumph and so, too, was England's victory in this Test. In 28 Tests he hit three other hundreds and his Test average of just under 40 was higher than his career average for Scotland, Kent and Essex.

He enjoys broadcasting and has proved a perceptive summariser in his distinctive voice which still bears a strong trace of native Ayrshire.

NORMAN DE MESQUITA. *Born 28 January, 1932.*

Long ago immune to quips about mosquitoes, Norman has, through a mixture of confidence, competence and breezy gift-of-the-gab, forged a highly successful career in broadcasting. Known best to listeners on BBC Radio London, he also does a great deal of freelance work, notably as Public Address announcer for a wide variety of sporting promotions including tennis and squash.

I first met Norman when we were both doing one minute reports for the long defunct south-east Saturday evening programme Sports Session, produced by one of BBC Sport's unsung but invaluable backroom men, Godfrey Dixey. Amongst our fellow reporters on football matches for that programme were Geoffrey Green of *The Times* and the famous Boxing commentator W. Barrington Dalby. Norman's work then, as it is now, was always thoroughly professional: he would give a well rounded description of the match with a touch of his own style and the essential facts all included in the strict minute allowed.

He has shown his ability in John Player League matches on Sundays whilst doing his own scoring, a considerable feat of dexterity apart from requiring great concentration. He is a man on top of his job. He also writes occasionally on cricket and football for *The Times*.

NEIL DURDEN-SMITH. *Born 18 August, 1933.*

Were he not a highly successful business man in the field of Public Relations and Sports Promotion, Neil Durden-Smith (who like Denis Thatcher and Kingsley Amis, is at least as famous as his famous wife!) would do more broadcasting than he does.

A good cricketer, he played for the Navy and Combined Services and was ADC to the Governor General of New Zealand, Lord Cobham, better known in cricket for his big hitting for Worcestershire and, amongst other things, his Presidency of MCC.

Other activities outside commentary boxes in recent times have included an enterprising and successful two years as Chairman of the Lord's Taverners, the charity based on cricket and cricketers which does so much to help physically handicapped people.

As a commentator Neil is smooth and unhurried.

RAY ILLINGWORTH. *Born 8 June, 1932.*
The insight and cricketing nous which made Raymond Illingworth such an outstanding captain was at once evident when he joined TMS as a summariser in the Headingley Test of 1982. Quick-witted and perceptive, he is also a natural communicator.

His achievements for Yorkshire, Leicestershire and England as off-spinner, batsman, sound fieldsman, and captain, are well known. Like Imran Khan more recently, 'Illy' became an even more effective cricketer when he took on the extra responsibility of leadership at Leicester and in 1970/71 he returned home from Australia with the Ashes regained, having, as always, made full and canny use of the resources at his disposal.

No cause was ever a losing one to Illy which is no doubt why in 1982 at the age of 50, he became official Yorkshire captain for the first time.

COLIN MILBURN. *Born 23 October, 1941.*
Only those who saw him play cricket before he lost the sight of an eye in a car accident in 1969 will fully appreciate what the game lost. If he had been humourless off the field and of average weight on it he would still have been a popular cricketer with spectators because he was a bold and attractive opening batsman who hit the ball very hard indeed in an orthodox way, delighting in the hook and the cover drive. Add to this his Falstaffian bulk and his merry and warm personality and you had one of the great characters of the game, popular wherever he went for Northamptonshire and England and very successful everywhere except the West Indies where he had a rather disappointing tour in 1968. But for the accident he would certainly have toured Australia in 1970/71, because he played outstandingly for Western Australia in the Sheffield Shield. At least Test Match Special and Radio 2 audiences can now appreciate his rich Geordie tones and ready humour, plus a knowledge of the game gleaned from fearlessly standing up to, and attacking, the fastest bowlers in the world in the 1960s.

PATRICK MURPHY. *Born 14 August, 1947.*
Irish as he sounds from his name, the accent which comes over the air when he speaks has more of a trace of the Midlands of England.

His main job was as a reporter on both radio and television for the Birmingham News Room but in his spare time he indulged his passion for cricket by writing for periodicals like *The Cricketer* and a number of cricket books, including the well received *The Spinner's Turn.* In these books he has revealed his thorough knowledge both of cricket history and, through talking to a lot of players, of the modern game.

He succeeded Dick Maddock as Producer of Outside Broadcasts in the Midlands and in this capacity has produced cricket broadcasts in that area as well as travelling south to help out in the Sports Room and introduce Test Match Special.

He has a fund both of cricket stories and of ticklish cricket 'posers', though none, so far as I know, concern a cricketer called Murphy!

PETER PARFITT. *Born 8th December, 1936.*
After 16 years with Middlesex as a high-class left handed scorer of nearly 27,000 first class runs, Peter now runs a pub on the Yorkshire Moors. Acquaintances in need of topping up their fund of stories call in there frequently and 'Parf's' latest tales are related far and wide. In common with great players like the Edriches and even Henry Blofeld, Peter hails originally from Norfolk. In a ten year spell he played 37 Test Matches, his last in 1972. His great sense of fun combined with his experience of the game made him a real asset to the Prudential Cup broadcasting team.

PETER RICHARDSON. *Born 9 July, 1931.*
The best of a talented family of Worcestershire cricketers, Peter Richardson shared many an heroic opening stand for England in the 1950s, notably in 1956 and 1957, just before Peter May's side took their crashing fall in Australia. He seldom let his country down abroad, where his sense of humour helped to keep colleagues going through thick and thin.

A solid left-hander, he lacked neither courage nor determination and of his 44 first-class hundreds, five were for England.

One of his many practical jokes was at the expense of a famous commentator, the long-suffering E. W. Swanton, when Peter complained from the field that he was being distracted by 'booming noises' in the commentary box. These were, of course, the well known resonant tones of the *Daily Telegraph* correspondent. It was interesting to hear Peter himself sitting in the hot seat during the Prudential World Cup. Jim must have been tempted to get his own back.

JOHN SNOW. *Born 13 October, 1941.*
One of life's competitors John Augustine Snow was, if his heart was in the cause, always a very good man to have on your side. His wiry strength and marvellous rhythm made him a genuinely fast bowler and he was particularly mean and effective on quick wickets overseas, notably in the West Indies in 1968 and Australia in 1970/71. Also a smoothly athletic outfielder, he usually made runs if they were needed.

One of his strengths was his intelligence – more than most fast bowlers – he was always thinking, seldom wasted a ball – and this thoughtfulness qualifies him well for the business of analysing a game of cricket. A man of few words, those words are, nonetheless, well chosen.

FRED TITMUS. *Born 24 November, 1932.*
The producer of TMS must have been a little anxious, when signing on Fred Titmus for some work in the Prudential World Cup, that he might be called away to play for Middlesex instead! The little wizard of curling, floating, drifting off-spin has played for his county (and briefly, incongruously, for Surrey) in each of five decades. In addition to his 2,827 wickets (157 of them in Tests) he has scored well over 21,000 first-class runs with six hundreds, and he has opened the batting for his country.

His ready, sometimes sardonic, sense of humour comes over well on the air and his pipe smoke at least adds variety when mingled with F.S.T's cigars.

PETER WALKER. *Born 17 February, 1936.*
An experienced extremely competent broadcaster and journalist with a wide knowledge of the game, he played for Glamorgan between 1954 and 1972. Peter is best known nationally for his interviews and presentations on BBC Sunday television transmissions, although in Wales where he lives his is a well known voice on current affairs as well as on sport.

Born in Bristol, but South African bred, most of his life has now been spent in Wales, his adopted home, but his accent still has its South African strains.

A very tall man, his cricket reached a peak in the early 1960s as Glamorgan were building a side which at the end of the decade was good enough to win the Championship. He played three times for England in 1960, against South Africa, and did the double the following season when he also took 73 catches. A brilliant and fearless short-leg, notably to the bowling of Don Shepherd, he took more catches for Glamorgan than any other player.

REPRESENTING THEIR NATIVE COUNTRIES

TONY COZIER. *Born 10 July, 1940.*
Tony Cozier is an outstanding all-round broadcaster and journalist who knows cricket inside out and communicates its dramas and delights with the sure touch of one of his countrymen's master batsmen.

The son of a well-known Barbados journalist, Jimmy Cozier, Tony knew what he wanted to do from an early age and so brilliant have been the performances of both the Bajan and West Indian teams in the last 20 years, the position he has earned, through graft and competence, as the foremost authority on West Indies cricket, has made him also a world authority.

Editor of the excellent West Indies Cricket Annual, his broadcasting style is based on the BBC's methods but has fitted equally well to TMS and Channel 9 television in Australia. There is a monstrous story abroad that Channel 9 pay better than the BBC!

Tony is an eager and able club cricketer himself and has played as a guest for many English clubs, most of whose opponents are somewhat relieved to find that he is not another black fast bowler!

FAROKH ENGINEER. *Born 25 February, 1938.*
A brilliant wicket-keeper, dashing batsman, masterly on the onside, and great enthusiast for cricket and for life, Farokh Engineer is a Parsi of intelligence and charm. He has made a home in Lancashire and travels widely as an executive in the cloth business but still keeps a watchful eye on world cricket. On the field he was an entertainer par excellence, always slick and stylish in his keeping and moving from wicket to wicket at the end of each over with a characteristic brisk, strutting stride, encouraging his Lancashire or India team-mates with a smile, a word or a gesture. His debut for TMS was in 1982.

JIM MAXWELL. *Born 28 July, 1950.*
Jim has a hard act to follow. Alan McGilvray's reputation was international and in Australia he is a legend. His was the mellow voice of Australian cricket. But Jim has had considerable experience with the ABC in recent years and knows cricket well. He played with success at his school, Cranbrook in Sydney.

MUSHTAQ MOHAMMAD. *Born 22 November, 1943.*

'Mushy' is a widely popular cricketer of brilliant all-round skill, the most versatile of the famous Mohammad brotherhood, four of whom played Test cricket. (The others were Hanif, Wazir and Sadiq). Mushtaq batted with wristy skill, devastating off his legs or through the covers if anyone pitched short around his off-stump. He also bowled accurate and well disguised leg-breaks and googlies. It is not really appropriate, however, to talk of him as a player of the past, because he still plays Minor County cricket for Staffordshire, accepts any chance to play the game anywhere in the world and, despite being a valued employee of Pakistan International Airlines, he would happily return to the talented Pakistan side of today (and hold his own in it) should anyone ask him. Perhaps it is safer, therefore, to say that in his 57 Tests so far he has scored 10 Test hundreds. He was the first Pakistan cricketer to score more than 25,000 first-class runs and he captained Northamptonshire.

BOB NIXON. *Born 18 November, 1924.*

Bob Nixon is a well known broadcaster in Zimbabwe and the increasing prominence of Zimbabwe as a cricketing nation since changing from being Southern Rhodesia has made it possible for him to become better known internationally. In broadcasting for the BBC in the Prudential World Cup he fulfilled a longstanding ambition.

His commentary on Zimbabwe's surprise first round win over Australia will be dragged out of the Archives regularly for many years to come. 'And you would think this was Harare or Bulawayo, but it's not, it's Nottingham . . .'

A practising dentist in Bulawayo, Bob was elected to the Zimbabwe Parliament early in 1983 as an independent.

ASHIS RAY. *Born 28 June, 1951.*

Like many intelligent Indians a studious follower of cricket, Ashis Ray has made occasional broadcasts for several years on the BBC World Service.

He was first heard on TMS in India in 1981–82. The commentaries then must have been a trial to the spirit much of the time, so slow, and turgid, was much of the play, but Ashis's typically Indian love of the game came through, and he made the very most of any drama that there was to recall, sometimes reaching a fever pitch of excitement as he debated whether the ball would go for two or three!

Hailing originally from Calcutta, he now works as a journalist in London where he obviously has good connections because when he recently got married, the Indian High Commission, no less, gave a party for his bride and himself.

ALAN RICHARDS. *Born 9 May, 1922.*
An old friend of TMS, Alan Richards made his tour of England with New Zealand in 1983, representing Radio New Zealand. A useful cricketer and footballer himself in his youth, he has commentated on both sports for many years and travelled widely following the fortunes of his country on the cricket field. In recent years he has had a much better story to tell supporters at home. Nor is he afraid to speak his mind, as I discovered when I covered the 1976/77 tour of India. The MCC visit followed immediately one by New Zealand. The visitors had been the recipients of what Alan was not alone in thinking were some rather harsh umpiring decisions. He had his say on the matter and when I arrived in his wake it was to find that a ruling from on high in All India Radio had decreed that no visiting commentator would in future be welcome as a regular member of the AIR commentary team! Alan, I'm sure, has long been forgiven and he may be said to have been ahead of his time in considering that umpires, in some circumstances, should not be immune from criticism.

LUCIAN WIJEYSINGHE. *Born 15 July, 1939.*
Lucian Wijeysinghe is a product of Royal College, the famous Colombo School. Every year Royal play a match against St Thomas's which is followed with the same intensity as the Eton/Harrow or Oxford/Cambridge matches used to be in Victorian times. Perhaps more so: the match nowadays is even televised. Not long after leaving Royal, however, Lucian came to England to take a job in insurance and is now an executive with a Birmingham firm. Indeed he has lived and worked in England for thirteen years and says he felt divided loyalties when England and Sri Lanka met each other in the World Cup.

A good cricketer and athlete himself, Lucian's younger son recently broke a junior record in the hop, skip and jump at King Edward's School, Birmingham, and shows promise also as a cricketer.

Wijeysinghe senior fitted easily into the TMS team for the world cup matches, helping everyone with the pronounciation of one or two of the longer names and with the identification of some of the lesser known faces. His heartfelt 'Well played Sri Lanka', when his country defeated New Zealand at Derby was echoed by all cricket lovers.

ENGLAND IN INDIA 1981/2

INDIA REVISITED – Tony Lewis

Indians wearing dhoti and headcloth; Indians in worn-out jackets and shiny winkle picker shoes; bearded Indians in patkas, the Amritsar look; Indians in sandals chewing betelnut; dutiful begums in saris and curly-toed slippers. Indians everywhere.

Indians carrying briefcases tied with string; Indians bearing four hold-alls at a time; Indians chattering Hindu, Urdu, or fast, lilting English; Indians wagging heads, calming screaming babies, squeaking old prams; Indians born to queue; Indians taught to grease the palm, shoving to the front, cheating the queue. Yes, it was good to be back at the Air India check-in at Heathrow!

Keith Fletcher's England were already soldiering in the sub-continent when I left. The time had come to pursue them with the tools of my trade – typewriter for the *Sunday Telegraph,* voice for Test Match Special, duty free whisky for me.

A camera crew went straight to the front of the queue. They announced loudly and confidently 'BBC Television News' as if it meant Open Sesame. It did. Michael Blakey, friend of many a campaign led me by the hand.

Tall and proudly handsome, Safraz Nawaz was promenading the Heathrow Departure lounge. I saw him about five times in the five hour wait, but he did not see me. Why was he wearing a different suit every time? Perhaps he was doing a Lord Lucan act; according to my newspaper he should be in Australia with the Pakistan side.

On the smooth flight to Bombay I read the sad announcement for cricket that John Henry Webb Fingleton was dead, aged 73. As I stared out of the aircraft window, recalling his 'G'day druid,' every time we met, a ten year old Indian was sick all over the floor. It was on the descent to Bombay. Still, Fingo would not have minded sharing the moment with that poor, heaving lad; it was confirmation that the cricket writer's passage to India has not changed.

I had better declare my hand. I love India and have the utmost affection, too, for Air India. I am not forced to write this because I was deified there for once leading a losing England Test Side. I even relish the scragging porters and taxi drivers at the Bombay air terminal. I swoon willingly to the stink of the Bombay swamplands, even the sight of a nation squatting at the roadside in response to the Hindu compulsion to defacate when the sun rises.

Of course ten years ago when I arrived with the MCC team I was feted with the rest of the lads. There was a headwagging official at every airport saying 'Wee Eye Pee, Wee Eye Pee, you are Wery Velcome.' This time it was a quiet car sent by friends and off to their apartment for half a day's sleep.

What news in Bombay? Most seriously the horse racing season had to be put back a fortnight because the sewage works on the far side of the beautiful course had overspilled and flooded the stables. Calamity. What is Bombay without the races?

Another newspaper paragraph caught my eye. There was speculation that the All India Radio commentator Raj Singh no less, was to marry the singer Lata; Lata the famous Maharastra Melody Maker, the Indian Piaf who had been crooning her way around Bombay for many a year. Raj Singh? I don't believe it. 'After a song from Raj Singh, it will be commentary from Don Mosey.' The commentary box will never be the same again!

I joined with sahibs Mosey and Baxter at Ahmedabad. They looked fresh and eager. It was early in the tour. I have never seen so much dew on a cricket ground, a thick silver carpet. I have never before been in a commentary position so tangled underfoot with cables. We commentated for an hour knowing that nothing was getting through to Britain. Engineers crawled around our seats plugging and unplugging. Wires and cables were passed under us, above us, around us. We heard Christopher Martin-Jenkins in London playing classical music and saying 'We are doing our best to re-establish contact with Ahmedabad.' We were a captive audience. We had been lashed to our chairs; all right if you enjoy bondage, but not so good if you want to go to the lavatory.

We did our hopeful chat into a microphone which looked like a small tubular cigarette lighter. Even as you projected the voice over the top of it you knew there was no chance that it was going anywhere but down the tube. Gallantly we kept up the repartee.

Eventually Baxter flipped. He lost his temper, which sometimes works in India, though patience and a feel for eternity usually works better. 'Whoever you are, stop shouting hello, hello stadium. Get off the line Bombay and let me hear London . . . Yes, I am Ahmedabad . . . You are not Ahmedabad, you are Bombay . . . I am Ahmedabad. How can you be Ahmedabad, when I am Ahmedabad . . .' It was all deafening stuff until Don

Mosey turned to Peter to reveal, 'My dear chap, you are BOTH Ahmedabad because you are talking to the Sikh engineer who is on the phone five yards behind you!'

I tried out the true Brit, stiff-upper lip direct interogative. 'Why is the microphone not live?' 'Oh! Sahib! Microphone more than live,' was the answer. I dropped it as if I was going to sizzle in my electric chair. C.M.J, by now awash with Chopin Waltzes, played on.

England won by five wickets. I met Govind Bawji my old bearer. He still looks after England teams, helped by two sons. He looked slimmer and fitter: quite the reverse of me. Govind used to protect his England captains and managers through the night by sleeping on a bedroll outside the door of the most modern hotel room.

In a long wait at the airport that night I made my first encounter with Ian Botham's giant transistor tape machine. Ian I like very much, his tape machine and choice of music I loathe. He insisted on assaulting everyone's eardrums with the noise of his own choice. John Lever sat close to it, nodding his head up and down as if he knew how to disentangle the cacophony.

However, I did read in a newspaper that Safraz had taken 1 for 44 in 10 overs in a day match v Australia at Melbourne yesterday. Oh! And by the way, I believe I saw Raj Singh blush as he denied a romantic link with Lata. Back at Bombay, Keith Fletcher was happy on the day his dad arrived. Jo Fletcher had come on the trip with his old pal, an 81 year old butcher from Melbourn in Cambridgeshire, called Arthur Leech. Astonishing Arthur arrived in Bombay from London at 5 a.m. and was bounced by taxi for three quarters of an hour through waking Bombay to the President Hotel. He put his feet up for a while before easing into a full British breakfast. Then with Jo Fletcher he took a taxi to see Keith and the England team at the Taj Mahal hotel. While Jo was blinking, half asleep in the scorching sunshine, Arthur was around the back of the Taj measuring for a new suit and bartering for ivory carvings. He then rejoined the somnolent Jo to take a swim and some sunshine. By supper time he was back at the President chivvying his travelling companion into jacket and tie for a curry supper and, insisting on going completely local, by ordering a bottle of Indian red wine. As everyone staggered behind him to bed at 10 o'clock he paused at the reception desk to book an early morning call and a taxi for the Test Match. How did he do it? 'First World War, y'know, Arthur was,' said Jo. 'Made 'em different, then.'

Alas the cricket tale from here on is not great reading . . . of an early Indian victory followed by five drawn matches which almost ground to a halt with slow over rates and slow batting. Somehow the tempo of affairs does not trouble the Indians and watching Tests out there was the usual crowded experience.

India must always be revisited, because of the cricket lovers. They are proud but unselfish and never spare the hard-earned rupees or personal comfort to get to their Test Match stars.

An excerpt from my diary. December 10, 1981, written from a room, high in the Asoka Hotel, Bangalore.

Bangalore is waking. No breeze in the tall healthy trees in the foreground which enclose the large hotel swimming pool. The sand-coloured tennis court is silent. No one moves around the outbuildings. Everything in Bangalore beyond these trees lies blindly asleep under the cover of a heavy haze. Birds caw and chirp and one is stuck on the same faint peep. The occasional horn sounds. It is 5.45 a.m.

At 5.30 a.m; to my left, a hundred yards or so away, across the road, the fairways of the golf course glisten. The city, towards the skyline is still shrouded. Bangalore would make now one of those impossible jig-saws of identical flat-roofed buildings, all the same colour, whose outlines are only broken by the thin trunks and the sprayed leaves of the palm trees. Perfect peace. I imagine that one or two England players across in the West End Hotel will be sitting thoughtfully out on a balcony, wondering what the day will hold; soaking up the quiet, the cool, the easy time while it lasts. It is the first morning of the second Test.

5.55. In the distance a train sounds the plain whistle of a kettle boiling. Then the split note chord blares through the mists from the same direction. There is no sun yet.

Suddenly I can see something moving in the distance, the haze is rising and through its filigree fringe a solid dark form is ever so slowly on the move; just to be sure, I have to measure it against a far off water tower.

6.00. Now I see more clearly. A long train is sneaking under early morning cover into the heart of the city. It blows again, the two note chord again. I know exactly which train it is, where it has come from and what its mission is.

6.05. The first sun is through. It shafts through the haze and strikes the brightest, whitest paint. Sides of buildings leap out of the picture as if lights had been switched on inside a dolls house. Elevations are clearer. The balustrade of the golf club opposite is bright, white icing on a cake. Now the gentle thud of tennis balls below me.

6.10 and the train blasts again and again, it is hissing closer and closer towards the hotel, almost on to the tennis court. The non-stop whistling now warns people off the track, clears the oxen, wakes up the dogs. A woman walks across her flat-roofed apartment opposite and spreads out the washing. The train is 50 yards from me, a mile out of Bangalore station. It is years since I was near a big locomotive which is straining to relax its piston strokes after a long journey.

The sun is up. The carriages are overloaded. Windows frame heads, shoulders, elbows, faces, eyes. How did they breathe all night?

The overnight express, Madras to Bangalore hisses and clatters slowly past me. Depart Madras 10 p.m – arrive Bangalore 6 a.m: the Cricket Special. No inconvenience at all for travellers when India are about to begin a Test Match against England.

It could only happen in India and it is good to be back!

PETER BAXTER'S DIARY

Saturday 21 November

After a 48 hour journey (most of that time spent kicking my heels in Bombay) I arrived in the late morning at the pleasant little airfield at Baroda 250 miles north of Bombay, and after some hair-raising taxi rides (which brought me a blessing from an old driver because I accepted his exorbitant charge without question – unheard of in India) I was at last among familiar faces.

The Motibaug Palace ground appeared to be very much the Arundel of India. There was the feel of an English festival match as I approached by way of drives lined by huge multi-coloured shrubs. The playing area was ringed by low stands with awnings or shamianas and one of these coverings sheltered the press box from the mid-day sun.

I was quickly introduced by Don Mosey to the problems of the tour. He had booked telephone calls to London for the early morning sports bulletins which would coincide with our afternoon session of play, but he was not full of hope that they would materialise, and after seeing that there was only one telephone on the ground which was in the players pavilion and constantly in use by all and sundry, I was inclined to share his pessimism. However, at the close of a long hot day we did make contact by satellite circuit from the All India Radio box perched above the stands on rickety bamboo scaffolding. It all sounded so normal at the other end – so far removed from the heat, dust and babble of an Indian provincial town.

In the evening the players and press were back at the Motibaug Palace itself as the guests of the Maharaja of Baroda, an old friend of Test Match Special, having acted as summariser on the 1974 series. In a magnificent hall in the palace we were entertained by a local classical dance group who enthralled us with the eloquent movement and glittering costumes of the traditional Indian art. Setting the seal on the evening was dinner on the lawn outside the floodlit magnificent facade of the palace.

Monday 23 November

The main feature of what was the last day of the match was a truly splendid innings of 73 not out by Geoff Boycott in which he outscored both Botham and Gower in brisk partnerships. The declaration came at lunchtime – incredibly 11.30 on the last day – but the match was destined for a draw.

Now could we make contact with London? Our plan was for Don to stay at the ground with the press bus which would not leave until they had all filed their copy, just in case for once our call at the ground really did materialise. I would go ahead on the team's bus which was leaving straight after the game for Ahmedabad where the first One Day International was to be played on Wednesday. After a bumpy 2½ hour ride I booked my call and eventually fell asleep waiting for it. There had been no success for either of us yet again.

The towers of the Motibaug Palace, Baroda, from the A I R box and Messrs Gower, Subba Row, Cook, Botham and Richards pose for Murrell and Underwood.

Tuesday 24 November

The playing area of the Sardar Patel Stadium was in magnificent condition with a huge concrete stand dominating one end and at the back of this I found our commentary position. It was virtually a cave, but a party of workmen was in the process of erecting an untidy skeleton of irregular wooden poles to drape with brightly coloured heavy material which would, apparently, act as our sound proofing.

In the afternoon I joined a party of players and press on a visit to the celebrated local mosque with the 'shaking towers'. Our drive through the back streets of the city was my first chance to witness the simple poverty-stricken existence of so many of the people of India. To affluent westerners, living a whole life in the dust and dirt of the street's edge seems an unbearable prospect. Peering into the open fronts of box-like booths I could see tailors sewing, men having haircuts and meals being prepared while animals meandered almost unnoticed among the scurrying people. And Ahmedabad is a prosperous city, we were assured.

A small morning expedition to the mosque had returned with the opinion that the towers did not shake, but my money was on Ian Botham. 'I'll make them shake' he declared, and the one remaining minaret duly trembled. (The other one was a broken stump. Had Botham been this way before I wondered?)

Wednesday 25 November

I arrived at the ground at 7.30 in the morning to try to sort out the communications. An extra hour or two in bed might well have been more useful, but I did have the pleasant surprise of running into a bleary-eyed party off the dawn flight from Bombay – Tony Lewis and Mike Blakey with his BBC Television news camera crew. (It was my first meeting with the latter pair, Derek Collyer and Ian Pritchard, who were to prove the life and soul of the tour.)

I established with All India Radio that I could use their telephone for my early morning reports, due to start at 5 a.m. U.K. time. I even telexed the number to London – but there was no change in my luck. Then came the problem of the commentary circuit. A tradition on these occasions is to be told that there is no booking for it and inevitably we went through this ritual as I became increasingly depressed at our prospects. Tony Lewis has already related the outcome.

Thursday 26 November
After a round trip of Poona, Nagpur, Baroda and Ahmedabad the press corps was to a man relieved and delighted to be back in one of the world's great hotels and as a newcomer to the tour I was certainly impressed by the famous Taj Mahal Intercontinental. But there was work to do. At the Overseas Communications Centre I tried to ensure that the problems of Ahmedabad would not be repeated. At the Wankhede Stadium I found our commentary box – an enclosed, air conditioned room at the back of the stand which seemed a bit too remote for my taste but was certainly roomy. The ground itself reminded me more of Parc des Princes in Paris than any cricket ground I had ever seen.

At All India Radio's offices in the afternoon I was taken ceremoniously into the commentators' pre-Test meeting. All the commentators who would broadcast the Test in English, Hindi and the local dialect, Marathi, sat waiting for their definitive instructions from the station controller. After the usual sweet tea refreshment this notable made his pronouncement. 'Gentlemen, we must be unbiased.' Everyone nodded wisely and departed.

Then it was my chance to discuss the BBC's problems. These seemed totally inexplicable to the AIR engineers. Why did these people need a telephone link to London as well as their satellite commentary circuits? How could anyone possibly broadcast two programmes at once? I tried to explain the difference between Radio 3 commentary and short reports for Radios 2 and 4 and they were at least prepared to smile indulgently at me.

Friday 27 November
Amazingly the telephone had, as promised, materialised and I was able to report on it for Radio 2 as scheduled. The commentary circuit came up five minutes early and it would have been easy to get light-headed. We had our moments as you always will on Indian phones. 'My name is Baxter – B for Bombay, A for Ant-eater, X for Xylophone. . .' 'Please, what is xylophone?' 'All right, X for breakfast if you like. I want to speak to Miss Watson – W for William, A for apple, T for char. . .' That was understood.

The cricket, too, was tremendous with Ian Botham seaming and swinging

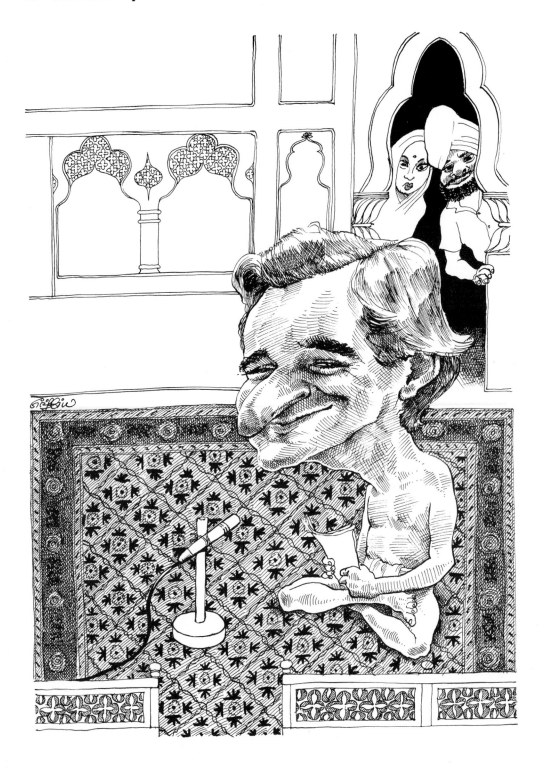

his way through India's batting. We felt rather cut off from the excitement in our air conditioned box, but we had a fine view of England's champion taking 4 for 72 in 28 consecutive overs as India were dismissed for 179 and despite the loss of Gooch before the close we felt it had been a good day for England and the BBC.

Sunday 29 November
The technical problems were minimal and we had a stream of willing volunteers from the England dressing room to act as expert summarisers. At least two of them were given a taste of some of the ancillary problems, though. Mike Gatting's chair collapsed as he was in mid-sentence and Paul Allott was greeted with a shower of pigeon droppings on his head as he took his seat. On the field the match was finely poised. India had a lead of 216 with one more wicket to fall. Botham had taken four wickets again, but Kapil Dev had been allowed to get away with an invaluable innings of 46.

Tuesday 1 December
After a rest day of speculation all the theories were quickly shattered. Far from being besieged by Indian spin, England were seamed and swung out to a humiliating defeat by 138 runs – all the harder to take after the last Indian pair had hung on for 35 minutes in the morning. The whole debacle was accompanied by barrages of firecrackers round the concrete bowl of a stadium and by late afternoon we were all back at the hotel.

Wednesday 2 December
Grasping the opportunity which the four-day Test result had given me I decided to assault the question of some microphones, sent to me by the BBC to improve quality. On the telephone the shipping agent seemed vague, so I took a taxi to the airport.

As I arrived at the cargo terminal at the airport with the agent, a pig was just leaving it. If I allowed myself to think that this meant that things would be informal, I was in for a shock. 'Have you got a TBRE?' the agent asked nervously. 'I don't think so,' I said. We arrived in an office where the man at the desk pushed a small crowd of people away as we entered. 'Wait half an hour,' he commanded imperiously. To me, after the agent had produced our shipping order, he snapped 'Passport.' Then, 'TBRE!' 'What is a TBRE,' I enquired. 'Downstairs,' was my answer.

On the lower floor we were given a form to fill in.'Wait five minutes' said the agent and disappeared. Half an hour later he reappeared, brandishing a wadge of papers which were his reward for filling in the form correctly. We went off to the customs hall the entry to which was controlled by a guard who wanted to go through all the paper. At last he stamped the latest wadge and declared, 'TBRE!' I really thought I had arrived. Within two yards I had to show it all over again.

Inside the customs hall a row of eight desks greeted us, each with two uniformed customs officers and a pile of paper. We went straight to the far end to my immense but premature relief. 'TBRE,' demanded the officer. 'Not until you tell me what it stands for,' I said. 'Tourist Baggage for Re-Export,' was the answer. Then we were away working our way down the line of desks at each of which the same questions were asked. Progress was slowed half way down the line when it was discovered that I was connected with the cricket tour. Cups of tea started to appear at every desk and the questions turned to include, inevitably – what did I think of Kapil Dev?

Suddenly the elusive package was thrust into my hands. I was euphoric for just a few seconds until I was led back to the first desk again. 'Not the whole lot again!' 'Oh no,' said my friend and sure enough we only called at two or three desks on our second run. 'That's it, then,' I said wearily. 'We still have the register to sign,' said the agent. That involved four more officials, but after two security checks to leave the building we were outside blinking in the sunlight. 'Why did you ask for the microphones?' asked my friend, amazed that anyone should volunteer for such a performance. Through gritted teeth I told him, 'I didn't.'

The day had gone and I had just enough time to get myself to the internal airport and the evening flight to our next destination, Hyderabad, 400 miles to the south west.

Thursday 3 December
There is an elegance about the city of Hyderabad which is the legacy of the celebrated Nizam, reputedly the richest man in the world in his day – and one of the most miserly. The All India Radio station, for instance, was the Nizam's former guest house, facing the domed and turretted palace across colourful gardens. Everyone at the station was helpful and I went through the usual tea-drinking routine before inspecting the ground with its lofty rooftop press box and the AIR commentary position situated in a groundsmen's dormitory. This threatened to be rather shocking for one of the AIR commentators, Chandra Nayudu, daughter of India's first Test captain, who was nervously contemplating only her fourth cricket commentary in five years.

Sunday 6 December
Before the evening flight to Bangalore for the Second Test we were able to enjoy two fine innings by Keith Fletcher, who boosted team morale with 108, and Mike Gatting with 71. Friendly telephone operators had fought well on my behalf. I overheard one exchange as one of them asked whether the transferred charges would be paid. 'Of course they will pay – it is the BBC!' How good to know that Aunty inspires such loyalty in Hyderabad.

Monday 7 December
Bangalore is known as a garden city and our hotel was evidence of this set in grounds heavy with trees and flowers. It also has a reputation as a military centre and provided Don with some nostalgia as he was stationed here in the war.

It was pleasant to know that we had two clear days before the Test, but I got the business of seeing All India Radio and the commentary box out of the way early on. The boxes were in a row – four of them – the highest commentary boxes I had ever seen, slung from the concrete roof of the tallest stand. Hospitably I was given the choice of boxes by my hosts. The vital telephone was there, too and Tony Lewis was installed in the nearby Ashoka hotel. Things were going well.

Saturday 12 December
England, in the face of a painfully slow over rate had reached 400 in the first two days.

At last my microphones, hard won through Bombay customs, were in use! Our engineers had installed them over the rest day at the request of the London end of the line. India answered the 400 soundly – 189 for 1 at the close with the inevitable Gavaskar there at the end having made 71 not out in the day. He was my interview target after play – a man I was to record many times on the tour and always a good subject.

Sunday 13 December
The news from home of a barely credible forty degrees of frost seemed strangely remote in Southern India, although we were able to tell those on the line that it wasn't all roses here. Sweaters were needed after dinner at Bangalore's altitude! However for some like Tony Lewis who would be leaving India on Tuesday it was worrying news and for all of us there was the question of how those at home were coping with the freeze.

Gavaskar surprised nobody by getting to his hundred – and on he went. The day was made more lively by a rapid Kapil Dev half century and five wickets for John Lever.

Monday 14 December
We had been very comfortable in the West End Hotel and so were sorry to check out in the morning before going to the ground to witness the inevitable draw. The only surprise in this was that Gavaskar did not reach his double century. We were also sorry to leave our very helpful AIR engineers who had worked hard to produce the right technical results for us and had performed the necessary function of keeping the numbers of hangers-on in the box to a bare minimum. (You can never eliminate them entirely in India.)

Now we were bound for the far north in two stages. This evening it was to be 1,200 miles to Delhi.

Tuesday 15 December
I suppose anyone who loves mountains as I do must long to see the Himalayas. My first sight of them was as romantic as I could have wished. Our aeroplane climbed out of pre-dawn Delhi bound for the north-west town of Jammu via Chandighar and peering out of the starboard window I

Scorer Kiran Mavani with Tony Lewis and Don Mosey at the KSCA ground,
Bangalore and another majestic drinks interval ends: this one at Jullundur.

gradually made out the dark jagged horizon in the pink rays of the rising
sun. They gradually assumed the forms of the mighty pinnacles as we grew
nearer and then we could see the sun glinting on the distant snows of the
mountains, tantalisingly out of reach as we descended into Jammu where
England was to play a three day game against the North Zone.

This was to be Jammu's biggest ever cricket match; we were greeted by
a band beating the life out of the unfortunate Colonel Bogey and we were
all garlanded before leaving for the hotel. We were given adequate
reminder that the uneasy border with Pakistan is only five miles away. An
armed escort accompanied us to the hotel and a column of tanks rumbled by
as we settled ourselves in.

Wednesday 16 December

Picturesque as the town was, the important question was – as ever – that
of communication. The night before our efforts had met with total failure.
Peter Smith of the *Daily Mail*, the leader of the press party, had received an
assurance that three telex machines would be on hand. On arrival at the
ground despite what was for me a heartening sight of three telephone
operators there was no sign of a telex machine. Smith protested. 'But we
have three machines,' came the came the affronted answer, 'One telex
machine three miles down the road and two men with bicycles!' I booked my
calls for the *Today* programme and waited to see what would happen. Total
failure.

Thursday 17 December

Don took over the reporting duties for the day as I gave myself the chance of a sight seeing walk round the 'City of Temples' as Jammu's billing goes. The nights and early mornings were very cold here – indeed everyone was making use of the electric fires in our rooms – but by lunchtime, with the sun high in the sky, it was hot enough for sunbathing.

Back at the ground, I found consternation amongst the press. The copy they had fondly imagined to be safe in Fleet Street as they laughed at my frustration with the telephone the previous evening had not, in fact, been sent until 11 o'clock that morning. There was now a lack of faith about the way they belaboured their typewriters.

Friday 18 December

Amused by the telephone problems a plot was hatching in the mind of our practical joker, Peter Laker of the *Daily Mirror*. In mid afternoon I received a call which was perfectly audible. 'Record us thirty seconds for the Radio 4 news,' I was asked. Amazed, I did so and then asked for a message to be passed to the Sportsroom with whom I had had no contact for several days. 'You're getting very faint,' said the voice, fading. 'You're fading, you're disappearing . . .' I smelt a rat. Laker's chair in the press box was empty. I watched the pavilion away to our right out of which in due course emerged P. Laker, as ever whistling and looking to the sky. 'Does this mean the Sportsroom didn't get my message?' I asked as he arrived with us, grinning from ear to ear.

Saturday 19 December

After another draw the day before, we had an early start for what was expected to be a five hour coach ride south to Jullundur. It was not an entertaining prospect, but it turned out to be very much more interesting than we had anticipated. At the border between the states of Jammu and Kashmir and Punjab the scenery changed abruptly. The harsh, rugged mountains gave way to well irrigated agricultural plains and the roads became long straight avenues of trees. Our main topic of conversation was the sweepstake on our arrival time and a yell of delight as the wheels stopped turning outside the Skylark Hotel told us that the correspondent of the *Standard* had triumphed yet again.

Sunday 20 December

Not having had the chance to see the ground the day before this second One Day International, I resolved to get there early. Taxis appeared to be non-existent in Jullundur, so it had to be the tricycle rickshaw method. This one was propelled by a character who looked so emaciated, that I considered suggesting that I pedalled while he sat in the back. I quickly found that his English was limited, too, as he delivered me to the bus station. Someone there helped me to put him right and we set off again, being overtaken en route by the English team bus, to the evident amusement of its inmates.

The chilly mist had not dispersed when we did at last arrive at the ground and I found the commentary box on an exposed concrete platform on top of a half-built (or half-demolished, it was difficult to tell which) grandstand. The view, though, was superb, or would be when we could get to it. The problem was that it required a ladder to ascend the last ten feet and none was in evidence. There were four such broadcasting platforms in operation, but eventually one bamboo ladder was found to serve them all and a 'ladder wallah' appointed to move it as required. I had some difficulty in persuading our engineers of the need for headphones, but they were eventually provided and wired into the equipment with the help of matchsticks. I found a telephone by courtesy of the local television service and amazingly my first call came up on time. Unfortunately there was a slight delay in my answering it, as the ladder wallah had chosen that moment for a tea break, but at last all was sorted out.

Tony Lewis had departed for England which had left Don Mosey the sole commentator for this match, but for most of the time his voice was given some respite by the badinage of Graham Dilley who seemed to enjoy the experience of sitting in as expert summariser. The mist of the early morning had persisted to reduce the match to 36 overs a side and in that time England made 161 for 7. During the innings Don described the ubiquitous kites overhead, but after looking at them through binoculars I established that they were vultures. Suddenly our commentary position felt very exposed! It was even more exposed as Gatting launched an attack of four straight sixes off one over from Shastri in his 70 not out, but his effort was in vain and India passed England's total with three balls to spare.

Wearily we headed for our coach and the daunting prospect of an eight-hour coach ride down the bumpy road through the night to Delhi.

Wednesday 23 December

By the standards of Indian Test grounds, the Ferosz Shah Kotla ground is tiny. But there was no doubting the usual fervour of the 30,000 crowd that jostled its way in, taking up every seat with half an hour still to go to the start. Our glassed-in box was narrow, but adequate, though as it was out of the sun the morning chill had not left it when we arrived. The technical set up looked efficient and there was a telephone close at hand. What a Christmas present!

Ashis Ray, no stranger to World Service listeners, made his debut as Don's co-commentator, nipping out at the end of each stint to do a spell on All India Radio and as if that were not enough he rattled off a report in Bengali for the BBC Eastern Service at the close. The players were well in the swing of helping our commentators out with their expert comments, but it was the manager Raman Subba Row who was appropriately at the microphone when Geoffrey Boycott made the highlight of the day, passing Sir Gary Sobers' record of 8,032 Test runs. It was a great personal triumph much appreciated by the crowd though they'd had to endure another slow day in which England made 190 for 1.

Thursday 24 December

England ground out another large total, trying to accelerate against an appallingly slow over rate and until the last three quarters of an hour it was desperately hard work. We had at least had the cheer of seeing Boycott's 22nd Test hundred and possibly more significantly, Chris Tavaré's first. What transformed the final period of play was Ian Botham. In just 26 balls before the close he made 47 not out including four huge sixes.

Our contribution to the Christmas excitement was to link Sir Gary Sobers and Geoff Boycott during the tea interval. Our Indian engineers were amazed and our scorer, Kiran Mavani, most impressed as Brian Johnston in London spoke to Sir Gary in Sydney and Geoff in Delhi. It was a satisfying coup on which to go to the Indian Cricket Board's lavish Christmas Eve party.

Friday 25 December

The only sign of Christmas so far had been the piped carols playing in the lifts, and it is rather difficult to imagine chestnuts roasting on an open fire as you head for a cricket match. This, however, was the rest day in the Test. So buck's fizz for the press in Frank Keating's room gave way to the press's own traditional party for the players. They had to drift away gradually to don their fancy dress costumes for the lunch party and we were able to enjoy the sight of two Clint Eastwoods (Lever and Tavaré) confronting each other. Some of the other get-ups needed rather more explanation, including Ian Botham's interpretation of Geoff Boycott, but we all enjoyed Raman Subba Row as Kermit the frog.

Sunday 27 December

Today's commentary had an element of excitement in it until the moment when India saved the follow-on. After that the prospect of a result receded with every run added in a fine 8th wicket century partnership between Shastri and Kirmani. Sadly, from a commentary point of view, Viswanath had been out before we went on the air for 107 denying Don and Ashis the chance to describe his brilliant strokeplay. The commentary was enlivened though by what was becoming a regular feature with the double act of Messrs Dilley and Allott teasing Don – a game that they (and he) greatly enjoyed.

Monday 28 December

Sterile final days were fast becoming the hallmark of this series. This one was also affected by mist to reduce the proceedings. At the end, the enthusiasm of the crowd laying siege as ever to the dressing rooms made the job of getting interviews all the more difficult, particularly as I had the ticklish subject of a rumoured row between Fletcher and Boycott to negotiate. This had been put to me as being 'all over the back pages of all the papers'. After it had been vehemently denied it was admitted by my colleagues in London that it was only in one paper.

Tuesday 29 December

When you think of a trip to India the sight you probably most hope to see is the Taj Mahal. This was our chance. Before dawn we were taking off on a twenty minute flight south to Agra, the ancient capital of the Mogul emperors. Today it seemed a depressed town but the hotel where we had breakfast was full of the luxury to attract the tourist. Before the Taj we were taken to the Red Fort of Akbar the Great. More splendid, if less well known, than the one in Delhi. There, from the marble tower where Shah Jehan ended his days, we caught our first glimpse of his great creation. Almost like a mirage through the mists of the Yamuna River shimmered the Taj Mahal.

If you imagine that you have really seen the Taj Mahal by looking at the lids of chocolate boxes or the brightly coloured pictures in Indian restaurants, you have barely scratched the surface. To come through the great gateway and see the great mausoleum filling the arch is an awe-inspiring sight. It stands against the sky as if it were glorying in its own splendour. As a tomb it has the status of a Moslem holy place and at the steps up to the plinth we all had to don overshoes before we entered the gloom of the interior. The actual tombs of Mumtaz Mahal and Shah Jehan are in a crypt below the more ornate replicas on the main floor. The jewels set in the marble flash in the light of the guides' torches. Outside again, the glare of the marble is almost blinding. Even these outside walls are set with semi-precious stones.

Immediately behind the Taj flows the sacred river Yamuna and most of our party flocked to look down on the gruesome spectacle of hundreds of vultures tearing the carcase of a horse apart – a stark contrast to the magnificence beside us.

As we took off from Agra we saw again the contrast – the Taj Mahal rising like an elaborate wedding cake amidst the dun coloured surroundings. Among the memories the slightly less than reverent words of Ian Botham rang. As he witnessed a staged fight between a cobra and a mongoose, 'That,' he declared in disgust, 'was the worst snake fight I've ever seen!' You get better ones in Taunton market any day.

Wednesday 30 December

Calcutta, the old headquarters of the East India Company, has acquired a reputation for pollution and overcrowding. During our drive from the airport late on the previous night it had looked like a vision of a Dickens novel with a large section of the population apparently huddled on the pavements.

My morning attempt to contact All India Radio was doomed to defeat at the hands of the telephone system, but rescue was at hand in the form of a visitor who announced himself as the Bengal Cricket Association's radio liaison officer. He guided me to the AIR building which turned out to be just across the maidan from the hotel. It was a pleasant, airy place, built, I guessed, before the war to cope with extreme heat without the aid of air

Left Our engineers at Jullundur enjoying the help of relatives and friends. *Right* Bringing the good news from Delhi to London – the Ferosz Shah Kotla press box.

conditioning. The office in the foyer where we had to wait was staffed by two sari-clad maidens listening to three transistor radios, each one carrying a different programme at full volume. I did identify a hockey commentary on one of them. 'Pakistan are leading Argentina,' I was told. The World Hockey Cup had started in Bombay on the ground where a month before the Test series had started.

Now my task was to explain our requirements for the Fourth Test, due to start on New Year's Day. In this I was grateful for the intervention of our scorer, Kiran Mavani – a native of Calcutta himself. Our need for headphones was constantly a source of mystification to our hosts, but Kiran spared my feeble efforts of explanation by relating to the assembled hierarchy how we had done the Boycott/Sobers link in Delhi. His enthusiasm and insistence carried the day.

Immediately next door to All India Radio was my next port of call – the world's second largest Test ground (after Melbourne) – Eden Gardens. From the glassed-in commentary box at the back of the towering new main stand, the groundsmen working on the pitch looked like ants. It was an awe-inspiring thought to look round at those lofty stands and imagine them as they would be on Friday crammed with 90,000 baying Bengalis.

Friday 1 January 1982

A new year and perhaps some hope for England to get back into this series repeating the win of Tony Greig's side in 1977. Keith Fletcher had missed that match with an injury and yet declared this to be his favourite Test ground. Like the rest of the side, he had been in bed long before the new year had been heralded in by a party of pressmen in the hotel. We had been joined by Raman Subba Row and the visiting President of the MCC, Hubert Doggart. Fortunately there were no thick heads amongst our party as our coach edged its way through the ant-like masses which converged on Eden Gardens.

Ashis Ray, happily at home in his native city, was alternating between us and the nearby All India Radio box to a schedule which called for a complicated commentary rota for TMS. We were joined for a time by David Gower, still full of self-recrimination for having got himself out with a rash stroke to the last ball before lunch for 11. At that point England were 68 for 3 but by the close they had improved matters to be 198 for 5 thanks to Gooch's 47 and Botham's 58 and to Keith Fletcher who was 46 not out.

Saturday 2 January
After a twenty minute discussion about whether the BBC's credit was good for a collect telephone call, I had success with my morning reports to Radio 2. The success was only partly muted by the decision of an Indian telephone operator to make her debut on Radio 2 in the middle of the first call. The afternoon's commentary was marred by a number of irritating line failures during most of which we could still hear the voice of Christopher Martin-Jenkins battling on valiantly. It was good to be joined in the evening session by an old friend of TMS – Pearson Surita, the great Indian commentator of the fifties and sixties. He and Don found themselves embroiled in an interesting discussion about the position of the setting sun in these parts. Don had made a remark about the pitch running north-south. 'Oh, no,' said Pearson, 'It runs east-west. Always has done!' 'In that case,' asked a mystified Mosey, 'Why do they leave a gap in the stands over mid-wicket to catch the last rays of the setting sun?' Pearson was not to be impressed by the scientific argument.

Sunday 3 January
It was inevitable that Brian Johnston would have heard and enjoyed the previous day's exchange with Don and Pearson Surita on the orientation of the wicket. 'Ah, Alderman,' he exclaimed when the tea interval's two-way conversation time came along, 'Do tell us where the sun is setting in Calcutta these days. When I was last there it was in the North!'

After India were dismissed for 208, giving England their first first innings lead of the series we were joined in the commentary box by the Middlesex duo of Mike Gatting and John Emburey who contributed to a lively last session.

Wednesday 6 January
We had discovered by this time what a polluted city Calcutta is. Coughing seemed to be the norm amongst the locals and many of our party, too, had picked up irritating coughs. On the rest day it had taken until early afternoon for the sun to pierce the morning smog, so the England camp had

been apprehensive that these sort of conditions might halt their progress with India facing 306 to win. In the event on this final morning of the match the mist was quite light. But Sunil Gavaskar as captain of India is a powerful figure, and although the umpires did make him go through the farce of facing one ball (perfectly middled) after his initial appeal, they eventually agreed with him that the light was unplayable. So, casting shadows on the ground as they walked, off trooped the players or at least some of them. Several of the England fielders stayed on the field making an obvious act of sunbathing.

Whether England could have won if they had continued, we shall never know. An hour and ten minutes was lost and England only managed to capture three of the Indian wickets they had needed to get back into the series.

Thursday 7 January
The rest of our party set off by train for Jamshedpur and a three day game against the East Zone, but after my morning return visit to the Calcutta Club I was off to Kathmandu and a three day break from the tour, leaving Don in charge of operations.

Sunday 10 January
After the rarified Himalayan atmosphere of Nepal the layer of smog which could be seen over Calcutta as we came in to land was somewhat depressing, but it was only to be for one night and the experience of Kathmandu had been a splendid tonic. We had taken the morning flight along the mountains to Everest, watched the sun set on the mighty peaks and turn them glowing pink, wandered the unspoilt streets of the almost mediaeval town of Bhaktapur and sipped rice beer from a brass cup in the quaint Nepalese equivalent of a pub.

The first journalists to return from the drawn match at Jamshedpur were eager to hear of the jaunt and it was only from one of their passing remarks that I discovered that I had missed the biggest story of the tour. Geoff Boycott had returned home. The official explanation was that it was by mutual consent between Boycott and the tour management. Secrecy had surrounded the departure at Boycott's request and telephone and telex problems had greatly hindered my colleagues. It was annoying to think that I had missed such an important event, not that I could have added any help had I been there. The next day, we were to fly 800 miles down the east coast to Madras for the Fifth Test.

Wednesday 13 January
This Fifth Test in the six-match series was vital for England. Failure to win would mean they could not win the series. Reports of the Kanpur pitch did not make a victory there in the final Test a likely prospect.

In our roomy commentary box slung under the roof of the Chepauk stadium we were joined by Peter Austin, an England supporter out in India to see three Tests, who was to act as our scorer in the absence of Kiran Mavani who had stayed in Calcutta. I had been accommodated for my telephone reports to Radio 2 on an instrument in the Telex office on the ground floor of the stand next door to the England dressing room. The problem was that there were no gangways through the packed seats to get there. I had to disrupt a row every time I left the box, so in the interests of Anglo-Indian relations I tried a different route each time. The telex office – when I reached it – was in a cage – a source of great amusement to the off-duty players who made gestures of offering me nuts like a monkey in a zoo.

Thursday 14 January
India celebrated the local Tamil festival of Pongal by batting all day without losing a wicket. They had already made a good start after being put in the day before. Today Viswanath was at his best making 181 not out plus a century, from Yashpal Sharma. As I interviewed Vishy at the close of play I looked at the little man wrapped in his pink towel surveying me with his bright eyes and choked as I remembered Don's description of him looking like the great Welsh actor, Hugh Griffiths. It was very apt, though I fancy Vishy might have outplayed that great man today.

Friday 15 January
It was no hardship for commentators to describe a magnificent hundred by Graham Gooch in the closing stages of the day. At the close he and Tavaré had put on 144 unbeaten for the first wicket and Gooch had 117 of them.

Monday 18 January
The Test match duly ended in the predictable draw after India had taken a first innings lead of 153 and then batted out time. My final interview with Keith Fletcher was recorded also by AIR. The engineer moving his microphone between the two of us nearly gave us both hysterics, but we made it.

Wednesday 20 January
We set off on the first stage of a thousand mile journey to Indore, where a three day game against the Central Zone was due to start on Friday. The morning flight took us from coast to coast and left us with another pleasantly relaxing afternoon by the pool of the airport hotel in Bombay before the next morning's dawn flight 350 miles north-east.

Friday 22 January
Outside the Nehru Stadium stands a large statue of Indore's favourite son, the father of Indian Test cricket, C. K. Nayudu. The aggressive stroke he is depicted executing, was nothing to what went on inside the ground. Ian Botham, it seemed, was not convinced of the value of a two thousand mile detour to play the Central Zone at this stage of the tour. He thought he'd have some fun. In doing so he gave the rest of us, including the smallest

crowd of the tour so far, a great deal of fun. His innings lasted only 55 minutes but in that time he made 122 – one of the fastest hundreds of all time – which included seven sixes and quite a few fours which only just fell short. Afterwards when I went to interview him, I had to wait while he finished two furious games of badminton!

The exhibition of explosive power rather eclipsed another remarkable innings by Mike Gatting. He reached a hundred in 111 balls and it was typical of his luck that this effort was overshadowed by Botham.

When I tried to raise London from the AIR box at the close of play with this news, all efforts were in vain. I was taken down the road to the radio station to continue the attempt from there. Unfortunately the first few hundred miles of the circuit were by a rather tenuous radio link to Delhi, never a recipe for instant success. As we did make contact, though, the link was made more difficult by the Delhi operator who seemed to feel it his duty to interrupt our difficult conversation by advising me to 'talk to London'. After the eighth or ninth occasion, he received a good blast of Anglo Saxon which silenced him and greatly amused the technicians at my end.

Contact and instructions established with London I was shown to the studio. 'We have given you our best studio, Mr. Baxter. It is our music studio.' The room was well carpeted but totally devoid of any stick of furniture except a solitary microphone in the middle of the floor on an eighteen-inch pole. So like a sitar player I sat there, cross-legged, to deliver my reports on England's 367 for 5 and Botham's magnificence.

Monday 25 January
Despite two very pleasant parties given by the Maharani of Indore during our stay and some fine England batting in another inevitable draw (including, on the last day, a splendid hundred by Geoff Cook) I doubt if any of us were sorry to be on our way again. The travel arrangements were a little strange as we flew two sides of a giant triangle to reach Bhubaneswar, 600 miles to the east.

This city, the state capital of Orissa, had been chosen as our base for the third One Day International at nearby Cuttack, because of better accommodation.

Tuesday 26 January
Anxious to be at the ground as early as possible to tackle the expected problems, I hitched a ride on the team bus for the 20 miles to Cuttack, which had been the subject of plenty of grim tales during the tour, so the Barabati stadium was a revelation. It was easily the best looking ground we had seen, with stands in good repair and freshly painted. There was a strange structure at one end which prompted John Lever to remark as he emerged from the coach, 'And bowling from the lighthouse end . . .' My amusement at this was curtailed when I discovered that our commentary position was to be on one of the many balconies of this tower.

Left Lighthouse? Clock tower? The pagoda commentary boxes in Cuttack. *Right* Ready and labelled. The commentary boxes in Kanpur.

Wednesday 27 January

Our next trip along the causeway road between the paddy fields from Bhubaneswar to Cuttack was at 7.30 the next morning in convoy with the team bus to take advantage of their police escort to the match. Our second commentator for the match was to be Steve Whiting of the *Sun* whom I had auditioned in Madras and who had met with the not easily given approval of Don Mosey for his efforts. Needless to say our position in the clock tower had been altered since the previous day but we settled in on our balcony once we had sorted out the inevitable headphone game. These had, as requested, been provided. But they were on a short lead at the back of the box and could not possibly be worn by anyone sitting at the microphone which might make for disjointed discussions with Brian Johnston in London. Eventually the engineers acceded to our request without understanding why with the usual highly technical series of twisted bare wires.

The game was certainly exciting enough for Steve's debut. Thanks to some remarkable hitting by Fletcher who made 69 and included a six over extra cover – not one of his regular strokes – England reached 230. Gavaskar decided his only chance was to risk a slog from the first – and it worked. He made 71 and India got there with four overs to spare.

Our drive back to Bhubaneswar in the wake of this defeat in the three match series was first delayed by power cuts in the telex office and then nearly terminated abruptly as our bus driver – encouraged to take a short cut by the police escort – found himself heading at high speed for a bridge obviously too low for our bus. Fortunately he hit the brakes in time and we retraced our route through the jostling bazaars of Cuttack.

Thursday 28 January

This was one of those days of frustrating delays as we made our way back to the centre of India and the Sixth Test at Kanpur. We first had to wait hours for the delayed flight which took us to Lucknow with the Indian team and then, in convoy with their coach drove agonisingly slowly for two and a half hours through the night across the Ganges Valley, celebrated as being bandit country. Road works and a sedate police escort seemed to be the problem but when another bus scraped the Indian coach as it overtook, our escort was off at full speed in pursuit. We came up on the scene as the guilty driver was being hauled from his cab by the hair and given some harsh treatment in the middle of the road. After he had been slung in the back of the police truck a volunteer was called for from amongst his passengers to continue his job. They seemed understandably reluctant.

Saturday 30 January

Our commentary box was a well appointed temporary structure though inconveniently placed at the far end of the ground from the dressing rooms. I was encouraged by the helpfulness of the staff at the telex and telephone office in a sort of brightly coloured tent behind our stand. Encouraged, that is, until I discovered as I waited for my first call that it had been booked as a fixed time telex message, which might not have sounded quite the same on Radio 2. However, after this point, we had remarkably little trouble in that direction. They did always call me to the telephone very early for each report and I had to keep abreast of the score just before going on the air by running across the courtyard and climbing half way up the scoreboard ladder to see what was happening.

It was a gloomy sort of day, but our commentary went well, with Steve Whiting warming to his task and Bob Willis volunteering for a long stint at the summariser's microphone as England made 213 for 3.

Monday 1 February

After a Sunday badly attacked by the weather, the rain had persisted all the previous evening and it was apparent that play would not be starting on time, but I had to be at the ground for my telephone reports. I found the telex office still in the throes of mopping-up. The flimsy canvas covering had filled with rainwater on the previous evening and started to split sending streams of water down on to the operators, machines, and eventually, on to the makeshift wiring, fusing the machines one by one. Repairs were under way. Happily the telephones were unaffected.

Groundsmen not normally faced with the problems of making conditions fit for play after rain did well to get things going straight after lunch, so Test Match Special began for once with the first ball of the day. The programme was evidently taking hold of our engineer, as, despite the fact that his English was limited, I heard him humming our signature tune!

England took their score to 378 for 9 declared due to Botham's 142, but after so much time had been lost a draw was the only likely result and the series would be lost.

Wednesday 3 February

After a sunny rest day which I, like several of the others, had spent looking round Kanpur and the relics of the Great Mutiny of 1857 when the city had the name more familiar to British ears of Cawnpore, it was inevitable that we should get up to find steady drizzle which delayed the start for an hour. India batted through the rest of the day to dismiss any thoughts of a follow on and an improbable English victory.

The evening was for celebration as the England team gave a party for those who had helped them on the tour. Whether the Indian team could have been included in that category is debatable but they were there as was our indefatigable courier, Charlie Pinto to whom we made a presentation for all his great efforts on our behalf. We had had a saying on the tour in times of stress, which had been launched by the *Times* man, Richard Streeton; 'If you sit on the banks of the Ganges long enough, the bodies of all your enemies will come floating past.' The convenience of the party was that it was on those very banks, and sure enough there was Dick staring at the murky water hopefully.

Thursday 4 February

Thick fog delayed the final rites of the Test series, but we did at last have the chance to commentate on a furious spell of bowling by Willis and an 84 ball century by Kapil Dev whose innings was ended by David Gower's first Test wicket with a variety of Spedigue's dropper. After five consecutive dead draws it seemed only appropriate that the second innings of the match should not have been completed this time.

Sri Lanka 6–23 February

Our tour of India had ended in Kanpur, a city with no airport at the wrong end of the country. By way of Lucknow, Delhi and Madras we arrived in Colombo nearly two days after the end of the Sixth Test. The island was welcoming, though, and heavy with the palm trees which give it its annual per capita consumption of 150 coconuts.

After four pleasant days in Kandy watching a draw with the Board President's XI we took the coach back to the steamy heat of Colombo for two one day internationals at the Singhalese Sports Club over the weekend. These were both cliff-hangers, the first going to England for whom Graham Gooch had the task of bowling the last over when only 11 runs were needed – this after a rather lucky innings of 64. On the Sunday it was Sri Lanka's turn to squeeze home by three runs after an abrupt final collapse by England.

Inevitably the prospect of their first ever Test Match had kindled tremendous excitement in Colombo. At the Colombo Oval there was great activity. Fortunately I spotted in time the temporary stand being erected in front of the commentary box and casually mentioned to the organising committee the fact that half the field would be hidden from us. They very efficiently lowered the roof of the stand and raised our position to the front row of the press box – not a popular move with our journalistic colleagues.

For this Test we were joined by Tony Lewis and Henry Blofeld so it was quite like old times to have Bloers making an early bid for inclusion in *Private Eye*'s 'Colemanballs' with remarks like 'Fletcher looking just like – Fletcher'. Sri Lanka's great cheerleader, Percy, carrying a huge flag round the ground gave Henry plenty of scope for diversion.

On the field for the first three days England put themselves in grave danger of being humiliated. Then on the fourth morning a spell of bowling from John Emburey (inspired, he later told TMS listeners, by some rousing and chastening words from the vice captain Bob Willis) brought England right back into the game with a vengeance and with clinical efficiency the batsmen wound proceedings up for a seven wicket win before the close of that fourth day.

Understandably the Sri Lankan dressing room was in a state of shock when I fought my way in there to interview the captain, Bandula Warnapura. We could only find enough quiet for the job in a washroom full of coconut husks. I was sorry not to see any member of the England team in there and indeed could not remember seeing an England player in the opposition dressing room after play at any point in the tour which seemed rather a pity.

At least that win had given us a triumph to end the long tour on. We did not know it as we lazed in the sun waiting for our long flight home, but we had all missed the biggest story of the tour which we might have tumbled to if we had heeded one slip. The Queen Elizabeth II had called at Colombo and as we had the fascinating tour round, one player's wife had pointed to a map. 'Oh look,' she said, 'It's not so far from here to South Africa.' A week later the news of the South African Breweries tour was out. We hung our heads, but still felt we had all earned our campaign medals.

INDIA v ENGLAND 1981–82
STATISTICAL HIGHLIGHTS. Bill Frindall.

1st Test – Bombay

Keith Fletcher became the 62nd player to captain England in official Test matches but only the third from Essex after F. L. Fane (5 times between 1907 and 1910) and J. W. H. T. Douglas (18 times between 1911 and 1924). If Fletcher had played in the 47 matches that he missed since his last England appearance in the Centenary Test at Melbourne in March 1977, this would have been his 100th Test.

England (102) recorded the lowest total by any visiting country in India and suffered their first defeat in eight matches on Bombay's three Test grounds. It was India's eighth victory in 59 Tests against England and seventh in India.

Ian Botham scored the 23 runs he needed to become the first England player to score 2000 runs and take 200 wickets in Test cricket. It was his 42nd test – fewer than either Benaud or Sobers had taken to achieve this rare feat.

Bob Taylor made his 100th dismissal for England to join the select company of Evans, Parks and Knott.

Madan Lal, recalled after an absence of almost four years – during which time India and Viswanath had played 35 Tests – returned his best analysis in Tests by taking 5–23 in 12 overs.

2nd Test – Bangalore

India began a second Test with a 1–0 lead against England for the first time. Sunil Gavaskar, who was on the field for all but four balls of the match, scored 172 runs off 476 balls in 708 minutes. It was the highest score in a Bangalore test and he became the first Indian to score four hundreds against England. His innings was the longest in all Indian first-class cricket by 63 minutes – Robin Marlar suggested that 10,000 Indians were born while Gavaskar batted.

Derek Underwood broke Fred Trueman's record of 53 wickets for England against India but had required seven more Tests. Curiously he dismissed numbers 1 (Gavaskar 172) and 11 (Doshi 0) with the second and sixth balls of his 43rd over.

Keith Fletcher became the 18th batsman to score 3000 runs for England. With Gooch and Lever he set an Essex record – although 19 Essex players have represented England, this was the first instance of three appearing together.

Geoff Boycott celebrated passing Cowdrey's record of 188 Test innings with a half century.

Bob Taylor held his 100th Test match catch while his opposite number, Syed Kirmani, gained his 50th cap.

3rd Test – Delhi

At 4.23 pm on 23 December, Geoff Boycott hit Doshi to the mid-wicket boundary to pass Sobers's world Test record of 8032 runs. Boycott had played 30 innings more than Sobers and batted over 451 hours – the equivalent of 75 six-hour days or 15 complete five-day Tests. He also became the 13th batsman to score 40,000 runs in first-class cricket and the second Englishman after Barrington to score 1000 runs against India.

India's total of 487 was their highest against England in India and provided the first instance in all Test cricket of a hundred partnership for the eighth and ninth wickets in the same innings. Both were records for India against England, Shastri adding 128 for the eighth with Kirmani and 104 for the ninth with Madan Lal.

4th Test – Calcutta

An estimated 394,000 spectators attended this match to set a world record for any game of cricket.

Kirmani became the first Indian to hold 100 catches in Tests and Fletcher the first Essex player to hold 50.

Gavaskar scored his 2000th run against England, a total he had already reached against West Indies. No other Indian has achieved that aggregate against any country.

5th Test – Madras

Fletcher was the first England captain to elect to field first in India.

Viswanath's 222 established a new highest Indian score against England, while his partnership of 316 with Yashpal set a new record in Anglo-Indian Tests and for India's third wicket against all countries. They provided the seventh instance of the same pair batting throughout an uninterrupted day of Test cricket. It was only the second time that England had failed to take a wicket in a complete day's play.

England employed ten bowlers in the second innings. Only Allott's absence through injury prevented them from becoming the third side to bowl the entire team.

6th Test – Kampur

Kapil Dev reached his second hundred in Test cricket off only 84 balls and shared in a record seventh-wicket partnership against England of 169.

Gavaskar, with eight wins and two defeats in 30 Tests as India's captain, emulated the record of Sobers who led West Indies in 20 drawn Tests.

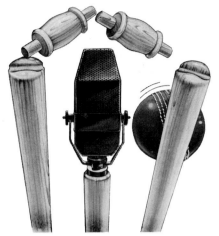

'DEAR BOYS IN THE BOX'

Brian Johnston

Every day when we arrive at the commentary box there are always shoals of letters waiting – divided into neat piles by Peter Baxter. I must say we are very lucky with our correspondents. The large majority write appreciative friendly letters. Those who have a complaint manage somehow to put it politely. It is unfortunately quite impossible to answer them all personally. We do our best to do so with those which cry out for a personal reply – especially those containing a stamped, addressed envelope! We also try to answer as many as we can over the air, either when it is raining or in a 'Listeners Letters' spot during the luncheon interval on Mondays. The others are all acknowledged on our behalf and the BBC's, by Peter Baxter – when he can find the time.

The trouble is that once a Test series gets started there is hardly any interval between the Tests, so that there is inevitably some delay. But we do appreciate the trouble which people take to write, and are encouraged by the kind things which so many of them say. But once again, I implore listeners not to send valuables like books, photographs, and old newspaper cuttings in their letters. If they could see the chaos in the box after we have all opened our letters, they would understand the reason! There is a great chance that something special might get lost.

Typical of the sort of thing which can happen, occurred in 1981. A girl named Karen sent us an amusing card for us all to sign for her birthday. I got all of our signatures on it, and then alas, could not find Karen's address – her letter must have been accidentally thrown away. So during 1982 I appealed to the unknown Karen to get in touch so that I could send her the card which I have kept in a drawer. What she must think of us I dread to think, but if anyone reading this happens to know a girl called Karen do please ask her if she ever sent a card to Test Match Special, and ask her to get in touch with us. I suppose by saying this I could risk hearing from twenty-three thousand Karens! I'll take the risk.

A big percentage of our letters contain requests for explanation of the laws and regulations. This question from Dave Blackwell of Hopwood Cricket Club is the one which we get asked most often;

> The batsman hits the ball back to the bowler *in the air.* The ball hits the bowler on the foot and then hits the top of the stumps at the bowler's end, knocking off the bails, with the non-striker well out of his ground. However, without touching the ground, the ball goes off the stumps straight into the hands of mid-off. Who was out? The striker caught or the non-striker run-out?

Rather illogically it is the striker who is out, although in fact the non-striker had been effectively run out *before* mid-off made the catch. And whilst talking of catches, I admit to getting this one wrong on the air when answering it on the spur of the moment.

> A ball is hit high in the air to an outfielder who knocks the ball up *inside* the boundary. Whilst it is still in the air he steps over the boundary but runs back into play again in time to make the catch. Is the batsman out?

I foolishly answered 'Yes', forgetting Law 32, Note 2, which says; 'A catch is fair if the fielder is within the field of play *throughout the act of making the catch.* It goes on to say that the act of making the catch starts from the time when the fielder *first* handles the ball. My friend, Don Oslear, was luckily listening, and kindly rang up to put me right.

Another one which temporarily stumped me was a question sent in by Gerry Crawley of Bristol, who wrote complaining that an umpire had given him out 'hit wicket' when, in hooking a short ball to the boundary, his toupee came off and fell on the stumps, removing the bails. The law says that the striker shall be out, hit wicket if, 'while the ball is in play his wicket is broken with any part of his person, dress or equipment.' The question was does a toupee come under any of these categories. I referred the matter to Donald Carr, Secretary of the Test and County Cricket Board, who has to decide this sort of thing. After he had stopped laughing he said that he was afraid that the umpire *was* right. Mr. Crawley was not only embarrassed – but out as well! Donald suggested that he batted bald-headed in future!

Another tricky one came from Leon Gouet of Harley Street, London. Shortly after the war he was playing for an Army side in Delhi. The field was near the local abattoir so there were dozens of hawks flying around. A batsman skied a ball a prodigious height, and as Mr. Gouet shaped up to make the catch the ball having reached its apogee, gently landed on the

back of a passing hawk. It flew on for a second or two before the ball fell off. But by this time Mr. Gouet was nowhere near underneath it, and so was robbed of a possible catch. But what he wanted to know was, if the hawk had flown over the boundary with the ball still on its back, would it have been a six? I see that in the letter I made a note that I had answered him over the air. But I cannot remember what I said! The fairest answer seems to me for the umpire to call 'dead ball' and not count any of the runs made whilst the ball was in the air.

Three other popular subjects among the letters are the excessive use of bumpers, the number of Overseas cricketers in County Cricket, and the noise of chanting and beer cans that has gradually become part of Test matches. As regards bumpers, Joe Cullum of Framlingham had a highly original idea. Instead of things like drawing a line half way across the pitch and leaving it to the judgment of the umpires, he suggested what he called a simple solution. Restrict the distance a wicket-keeper may stand behind the stumps. This would certainly mean that a lot of bouncers would sail over his head for four byes. But if he stood too close to a genuine fast bowler, I am afraid his hands would soon be badly bruised, so its not really feasible.

The T.C.C.B. are gradually dealing with the excessive number of Overseas players, but the noise problem is more difficult. I do sympathise with listeners who say that it ruins the broadcasts. But it is a free country and it is impracticable to tell people to restrict their enthusiasm. The only comfort is that the grounds in England are still far quieter than in countries like West Indies, India and Pakistan.

We also get hundreds of letters asking us quiz questions which we try to answer. I remember that this one from Clive Broadfield stumped us all at the time, though now that I have read it again, I think I have half an answer. The question was; 'Which bowler pulled a muscle whilst bowling and continued for the next six overs using a runner?'

At first glance, it looks complete nonsense. How *could* a bowler have a runner to bowl for him? But wait a moment. If, as soon as the bowler pulled his muscle, the opposing captain had declared, the bowler might then have been sent in as an opening bat with a runner. A possible solution. But whether it ever happened and who the bowler was, I just don't know.

Our mail always has its fair share of poetry, some of which we read out. The following ode from Anne Tomlinson of Weybridge is particularly apt after the dreadful start to the 1983 season;

Blowing, flowing hedges as the rain beats down
Pale, grey, undersides of leaves that swish and drown
Birds darting, low and swiftly to the shed
Through silver mobile curtains, dripping wet.
And in the road the traffic swishes by,
The rippling pools in gutters splashing high,
And squelching people trudging through the rain,
Monsoon? No – June – and Test Match time again!

I was naturally delighted to receive a number of congratulatory poems on my 70th birthday which I celebrated at the Old Trafford Test. Archie Reid of Glasgow sent me a short extract from one that was sent to him when he reached 70, and he thought it applied to me, too;

> We know that to ordinary men
> The span is three score years and ten
> And although to-day you've reached that score,
> You're good at least for twenty more
> But when at last an unkind fate
> Directs you to the Pearly Gate
> We're sure to Peter you will say
> 'Any cricket on to-day?'

But the one which gave me most pleasure, but which I did not dare to show to the others, came from Joe Green of Hull;

> 'I understand you are seventy
> I cannot believe its true
> The Alderman, Boil and F.S.T.
> All look far older than you!'

Encouraged, no doubt, by my well known love of corny jokes, we get sent a large variety of them, and the following are some of the better (???) ones!

> 'If Fred Trueman was standing naked in a snowstorm, what animal would he like to be?
> *Answer:* A little 'otter.' (Apologies to all concerned!)

> 'Who was the ice cream man in the bible?
> Walls of Jericho.'

After telling the above at Headingley in 1982 I received a letter from Peter Thorne of Chigwell, asking;

> 'What about L(y)ons of Judah?!!'

Someone else asked if I had heard of the Irish harpoonist who won the Miss W(h)ales contest! And finally, a delightful cartoon by Roy Davis of Eastwood in Essex. It shows a batsman bursting into flames when a ball hits the matches in his trouser pocket. He is also shown receiving the award of 'The Man of the Match'.

I cannot quite remember how it started, but I think a fielder had (inexcusably) given the two-fingered V-shaped salute to a section of the crowd who had been barracking him. Anyway, I know I asked the others in the box if they knew the origin of this rude gesture. Nobody knew and, as so often happens, in our mail the next day were a couple of letters giving the explanation. One of them was wrong, but Mr. Dempster of Southport gave the correct answer. Before the battle of Agincourt in 1415 the French vowed that they would cut off the two 'drawing' fingers of the English bowmen after England had been defeated. Instead, of course, the French lost the battle and it was *they* who got their come-uppance. As the French prisoners were being led away the English bowmen held up their two fingers to show that they were still intact, and ever since this has been a gesture of contemptuous defiance. The things one learns at cricket! We often hear about unusual cricket matches. During the third Test against India in 1982, their Captain, Gavaskar, had to retire hurt with a broken shin-bone, the result when fielding, of a typical Botham blow. Although he was so badly hurt I conjectured whether, if necessary, he would come out to bat on crutches.

This prompted Mr. Bennett of Hartley Wintney to write and tell us that in the Cricketers Manual by 'Bat', published in 1851, there was a report of a match played in 1850 at The Oval between eleven Greenwich pensioners, each with one arm, against an eleven of other pensioners with one leg apiece. Not surprisingly, perhaps, the legs won by one wicket. With two hands they could presumably hit fours and make catches, though how they were able to bowl is not related. Another item in the book mentioned a Westmoreland youth named Walker who, although losing both hands in an accident at a paper mill, played in a match with astonishing skill. He could do almost anything [*sic*] except bowl!

Mr. Wedge of Edmonton wrote and told us how he and some colleagues whilst waiting for a train played cricket on a snow-covered platform in Leningrad Station. A convenient tree was the wicket, a frozen snowball the ball, and an umbrella the bat. The temperature was 14° centigrade, but luckily they all had fur hats with the ear flaps pulled down – a very effective helmet. Naturally the Russians thought these mad Englishmen even more eccentric than usual.

Dennis Blake was responsible for raising a team to play the R.A.F. in Tangier. They used a piece of rough land given by the Sultan and as they had no mower, they employed twenty Moroccan ladies – called Fatimas – to pick off the grass by hand. Players had to be innoculated against tetanus and some used to wear a Jellaba – a loose hooded cloak worn by Arabs. These made it difficult for the umpire to give an lbw decision! One of my nicknames which I so often give to people puzzled Elizabeth Blatherwick of Walsall. 'Why do you call David Constant "the nymph"', she asked. Well, many years ago, in the late 'twenties, there was a famous play by Margaret Kennedy called 'The Constant Nymph' in which, incidentally, Noel Coward played. I was able to answer that one over the air, but I could not answer Geoffrey Drake of Shipley. Like scores of others he asked why we always refer to the score of 111 as the dreaded Nelson? He admitted that Nelson had one eye and one arm, but certainly had two legs. So what does the other one stand for? I am afraid I had to leave that one to Mr. Drake's imagination.

As a result of our conversations during the rain we often obtain interesting information. At Old Trafford last year we were talking about the condition of the outfield, and I was lamenting that my own lawn was full of dandelions and that I did not know how to get rid of them. The next day Desmond Bennett of Woodford Green wrote and gave us the cure which he had learned at school fifty years ago. Any boy discovering a dandelion had to report it to the cricket professional. He would then attend with a bottle of sodium chlorate solution and a meat skewer. He would then make a hole down the centre of the dandelion stalk, and pour the solution in. It was evidently a very effective cure.

I am the proud President of a club which has only two other members. It is called The Boaters Club and was started by Roger Eilson and Pat Hodges. They are two ardent Essex supporters and follow them round for all their cup matches wearing straw boaters, sporting a hat-band in Essex colours. They very kindly wrote to me asking if I would be their President which I gladly accepted. I don't have to do anything not even wear a boater though I happen to own one – rather like Bud Flanagans. It's all turned up in front due to a ball hitting it when I was playing in a charity match for Terry Wogan. But I do have the tie – dark blue with a golden boater over three stumps. I often wear it and meet my two other members for the odd drink at The Tavern. The tie puzzles people, especially as the boater looks rather like a flying saucer. But I like it!

And finally, we have some regulars who send us in Pun Songs. Cathy Downing, John Moody, D. B. Gardner and Brian Orchard are the most prolific. Here are some examples of their suggested titles, but please. . . DON'T BLAME ME!

Amazing GRACE
I'm GARNER wash that man right out of my hair
THE LLOYDS my shepherd
Try a little ten DENNESS
AMISS you since you went away
Thank EVANS for little girls
Happy days ZAHEER again
Keep BRIGHT on to the end of the road
Don't DILLEY dally on the way
KANHAI forget you
HUGHES are my heart's delight
Onward, CHRISTIANI soldiers MARSHing ASIF to WARR

BUT PLEASE, PLEASE . . . DON'T BLAME ME

Good-Bye for Now. Here's to the next time!

THE SUMMER OF THE ALL-ROUNDER
Trevor Bailey

After the thrilling summer of 1981, when a Botham inspired England came back from the dead to retain the Ashes, it always seemed probable that international cricket in 1982 would prove a big anticlimax, and so it was. However, there were additional reasons why it was a season which will soon be forgotten.

First, split tours with three Tests against each country can never expect to generate the same interest and excitement as a five-match rubber. After all, it frequently takes a visiting side a couple of tests to become acclimatised to our conditions, while if they encounter a bad spell of weather, they will probably reach their peak just when it is time to return home.

Secondly, India, who had just won an exceptionally dull series against England the previous winter, simply did not possess an attack which, in normal circumstances, was strong enough to beat our second XI, in England. The outcome was that the new England captain, Bob Willis, won the series one nil, with the second Test ruined by rain, while he made no serious effort for victory on the last day of the Third, on a very friendly pitch.

Thirdly, although Pakistan were both stronger and had more appeal, they certainly did not have the drawing power of Australia, or the West Indies. Their lack of adequate seam support for Imran, injuries, and an inexperienced captain were responsible for them losing a rubber they really could have won.

Finally, although the strongest possible England team had serious weaknesses, due to a shortage of quality bowlers in 1982, it was weakened still further by the ban on all those who had taken part in the South African adventure, because the countries were frightened the West Indies, India and Pakistan might refuse to tour and that could cost a great deal of money. The loss of Graham Gooch, one of the most attractive stroke players in the world was especially sad.

Keith Fletcher, who skippered Essex with skill and success for many years, was brought back to international cricket in the winter of 1981–82 and given the difficult appointment of taking England to India. A disappointing tour resulted in the new Chairman of Selectors, Peter May, summarily dismissing him, without giving him the opportunity to show his worth in England, where the odds of beating both India and Pakistan were good. Instead the job was entrusted to Bob Willis, who did the necessary, and in fact did not lose a match, as England's one defeat by Pakistan was under David Gower at Lord's, Bob being injured. This loss was directly due to our selectors who provided David with a completely unbalanced attack, consisting of four right-arm medium-paced seamers, and a flat off-spinner, which meant that though he could, and did, change his bowlers, he could not change the bowling.

Although the quality of much of the cricket in the Tests was below what is expected at international level, spectators did have the opportunity of comparing the merits of the three most successful Test all-rounders, Ian Botham, Kapil Dev and Imran Khan, their respective countries have ever produced. Never before have a trio of such outstanding all-rounders played Test cricket in the same summer. To make it even more fascinating, each did his utmost to demonstrate that he was the best in the world, an unofficial title clearly held by Ian Botham for his 1981 deeds against the Australians, and his figures in international cricket.

My definition of a genuine all-rounder is a player who is worth his place for both his batting and his bowling, as distinct from a batsman, who can take wickets, or the bowler who has the ability to score runs. There is no problem being an all-rounder in school and club cricket, but it becomes increasingly difficult to fill both roles in first class cricket, while it becomes something of a rarity at international level. Frequently, the county all-rounder is not quite good enough in either department, so that Selectors are forced to settle for a batting specialist, who can turn his arm over, or bowling specialist, who can make runs.

What made this trio of all-rounders so unusual was that each member was not only worth automatic selection for his country, in either capacity, but he was also the main strike bowler, an exceptionally attractive batsman, and a brilliant all purpose fieldsman.

How did Ian Botham, Kapil Dev and Imran Khan compare in the summer of 1982? The first thing which should be taken into account, was that India were clearly the weakest of the three countries, who only won one match on the tour, and never looked capable of achieving anything better than a draw against England in a Test. Their attack was anaemic, as their spinners lacked the necessary penetration and their seamers failed to provide

Ian Botham – attacking bowler and match-winning batsman.

adequate support for the admirable Kapil Dev, whose 10 wickets cost him 43 runs apiece. As a batsman he scored 292 runs in spectacular, swashbuckling fashion for average of 73. In contrast Ian Botham captured 9 wickets in fewer overs for less runs and made over 400 runs, including two centuries and an average of 134, but Kapil Dev was chosen 'Man of the Series', because he had to work harder for both his runs and his wickets.

Kapil Dev's pace was sharp rather than really fast, but he was quick enough, and tall enough to force most batsmen on to their back foot. He had a good high flowing action, a sensible run up and plenty of stamina. This enabled him to keep going for very long spells, though this inevitably meant that he lost some of his edge. I would rate him as the best pace bowler India have produced, as well as being one of their most exhilarating batsmen, who was only too keen to accept the challenge of bouncers from Willis and Botham irrespective of the situation. He certainly hit with enormous zest, whether with as much power as the redoubtable Botham must be a matter of opinion, but it would be true to say with more elegance.

Imran Khan also won the 'Man of the Series' ahead of Ian Botham and there can be no question that in these three Tests his all-round worth was greater than Ian Botham's and if he had shown the same acumen as skipper, as he did batting and bowling, Pakistan would have taken the rubber. He took a remarkable 21 wickets at 18 apiece in the three Tests, and also scored over 200 runs, averaging 53, invariably when they were most wanted. Against this Ian's 18 wickets cost over 26 and he only averaged 27 with the bat.

If one had examined the Test figures of Imran Khan and Botham before the series, one might have been surprised at the outcome, because the latter, though younger, had been considerably more successful with both bat and ball. However, as usual the statistics fail to tell the full story. They do not show the number of Tests which Imran missed when he joined the World Series and when both wickets and runs were much easier to obtain in Test cricket because so many of the best players were missing. It was also true to say that Pakistan were not nearly so dependent upon Imran to produce big scores, as they had a stronger batting line up than England, while conversely Imran never enjoyed seam support of the same calibre as Botham had with England. In addition, Ian played more Tests in England where conditions are far more favourable for pace bowling than the majority on which Imran had to operate.

Imran is a genuine quick bowler, among the fastest in the world with a slightly open action, whose natural ball tends to swing into a right-hander, but he has learned how to make it hold its own and occasionally leave the bat. Unlike Ian, his pace is sometimes on its own sufficient to obtain wickets. In contrast Ian is an attacking medium-fast bowler, who not only can swing the ball both ways and into the bat, but has appreciated the value of maintaining full length. A half-volley which swings late is a potential taker of wickets, especially in Tests. He has a busy approach, exceptional stamina which enables him to bowl very long spells, a useful bouncer, and is always experimenting. As a result, he is a relatively more effective bowler in Test cricket where dismissing the opposition is all important, than in limited overs cricket when the denial of runs is often the main objective. His problem in 1982 was that he lost much of his power of penetration and this spilled over into the Australian tour. The differences which were to be found in their bowling, also applied to their batting. Imran is an accomplished, basically correct player with a sound defence and a wide range of strokes. I have no doubt that if he had not been such a brilliant bowler he would have established himself as one of the foremost batsmen in the world. In my opinion, Ian is the finest and most exciting scientific hitter cricket has produced, certainly in modern times.

His strength enables him to mis-hit a six, his defence is sound and he is quite capable of playing a perfectly orthodox innings like other ordinary batsmen providing he resists that little voice which is always liable to whisper 'Now' to him. However, he can also do something which they cannot. He can sometimes, but not always, win a match, demoralise the opposing bowlers and execute a whole series of powerful and improbable strokes in a way which only Collis King could even approach. 1982 may not have been a great summer but it will be long-remembered for the great skills of three world-class all-rounders.

THEIR TEST MATCH RECORD IN THE 1982 SERIES

BATTING (* not out)

		Tests	Innings	Not Outs	Highest Score	Runs	Average
I. T. BOTHAM	v Ind	3	3	0	208	403	134.33
	v Pak	3	6	0	69	163	27.16
	Totals	6	9	0	(208)	566	62.88
KAPIL DEV		3	4	0	97	292	73.00
IMRAN KHAN		3	5	1	67*	212	53.00

		100s	50s	Minutes	Balls	6s	4s	Runs/ 100 balls
I. T. BOTHAM	v Ind	2	1	598	500	7	46	81
	v Pak	0	2	425	322	0	21	51
	Totals	2	3	1023	822	7	67	69
KAPIL DEV		0	3	351	272	6	40	107
IMRAN KHAN		0	2	627	460	5	25	46

BOWLING

		Overs	Maidens	Runs	Wickets	Best Analysis	Average
I. T. BOTHAM	v Ind	93.3	16	320	9	5–46	35.55
	v Pak	150.5	33	478	18	5–74	26.55
	Totals	244.2	49	798	27	(5–46)	29.55
KAPIL DEV		133	21	439	10	5–125	43.90
IMRAN KHAN		178.1	48	390	21	7–52	18.57

		5 Wkts in Innings	Balls per Wicket	Runs per 100 Balls	No Balls	Wides
I. T. BOTHAM	v Ind	1	62	57	2	3
	v Pak	1	50	53	2	7
	Totals	2	54	54	4	10
KAPIL DEV		1	80	55	19	0
IMRAN KHAN		2	51	36	2	21

FIELDING

Ian Botham held two catches – one in each series. Neither Kapil Dev nor Imran Khan held a catch in their respective series against England.

BILL FRINDALL

Kapil Dev – 'Man of the Series.'

ENGLAND v INDIA 1982 STATISTICAL HIGHLIGHTS

1st Test – Lord's

For the first time since 1951–52 England employed four captains within a period of twelve months, with Botham, Brearley, Fletcher and Willis following the earlier sequence of F. R. Brown, N. D. Howard, D. B. Carr and L. Hutton. Willis became the fourth Warwickshire player to lead England after the Hon. F. S. G. Calthorpe, R. E. S. Wyatt and M. J. K. Smith. At 6ft 6in he was the tallest Test captain since A. W. Greig (6ft 7½in).

Syed Kirmani, the only Indian to make 100 dismissals in Tests, played his first Test match in England after appearing in 54 in other countries. Deputy to F. M. Engineer in 1971 and 1974, he was not selected for the 1979 tour.

Kapil Dev took his 150th Test wicket (Tavaré) and recorded five wickets in an innings for the eleventh time in 39 Tests.

Edmonds (64) and Willis (28) registered their highest Test scores, and Randall achieved his first Test hundred in England after twice reaching 150 in Australia.

England's last four wickets added 267 runs with record seventh (125 – Randall/Edmonds) and tenth (70 – Allott/Willis) wicket partnerships for England against India.

Willis took his 250th Test wicket when he dismissed Malhotra.

Imran Khan – the other 'Man of the Series.'

2nd Test – Old Trafford

Ian Botham celebrated his 50th Test match with his tenth hundred – his second in successive Test innings at Old Trafford.

Sandeep Patil (129 not out) recorded the highest score for India in Manchester. By scoring 24 runs off Willis's 17th over – his second with the second new ball – he established a record for the most runs off an over in a Test in England. His six boundaries in that over (4, 4, 4 off a no ball, 0, 4, 4, 4) set a world Test record.

Kapil Dev reached his fifty off only 33 balls.

Gavaskar set a Test record by leading his country in 21 drawn matches.

3rd Test – The Oval

Ian Botham (208) achieved his first double century for England and his country's sixth such score against India – all have been compiled in England. He reached his 200 off 220 balls – arguably the fastest at Test level in terms of balls received – and set a new series aggregate of 403 runs for England against India in England.

Kapil Dev became the fourth Indian to take 50 wickets against England when he dismissed Tavaré.

The partnership of 130 between Kirmani and Kapil Dev, who scored 97 off 93 balls, was a record for India's sixth wicket against England.

ENGLAND v PAKISTAN 1982 STATISTICAL HIGHLIGHTS

1st Test – Edgbaston

Imran Khan (7–52) established a record analysis for Pakistan against England in either country.

Chris Tavaré, who made his debut in 1974 and was playing his 283rd innings, scored his 10,000th run in first-class cricket when he reached 19 in the first innings.

With 105 out of England's 188 for 8, Derek Randall was responsible for 55.85% of the total while he was at the wicket.

Tahir Naqqash had a spell of 5 for 20 from 45 balls.

Bob Willis celebrated becoming the first specialist fast bowler to play 100 innings in Test cricket by registering his highest score of 28 not out. He also extended his world record of not out innings in Tests by 245.

2nd Test – Lord's

Lord's equalled the record held by the Melbourne Cricket Ground by staging its 74th Test.

David Gower became the second Leicestershire player after Ray Illingworth to captain England. The last left-handed batsman to do so was John Edrich when he deputised for Mike Denness at Sydney in January 1975.

Mohsin Khan recorded the eighth double century in Tests at Lord's and the first since 1949. He became the second after Zaheer to score 200 for Pakistan against England and only the seventh (10 instances) to reach that total in all his country's 122 Tests.

In England's first innings of 227, extras (46) were top scorer for only the fifth time in 932 Tests. The total of 13 wides constituted a new Test record.

England followed on for only the second time in 35 Tests against Pakistan.

Tavaré spent 67 minutes before scoring his first run but eventually reached his 1,000 for England in 16 matches. By spending 60 minutes with his score at 24, he provided the first recorded instance of a player failing to score during two separate hours of an innings. His 50 took 350 minutes – the second slowest on record in first-class cricket.

Pakistan gained their second victory against England with 4.5 overs to spare.

3rd Test – Headingley

For only the third time in 31 three-match series in England, each side had gained a victory in the first two matches. England emulated their predecessors against Australia in 1888 and 1896 by winning the deciding match. It was their eighth win in their last 15 matches at Headingley. During that period they suffered just one defeat – by West Indies in 1976.

Majid Khan overtook Hanif Mohammad's record Pakistan aggregate of 3,915 runs when he scored 16.

IN THE COURSE
OF RESEARCH

Bill Frindall

'Who is the taller, Bearded – Gavaskar or Viswanath?'

Answers to Johnstonian conundrums like that have to be anticipated and found before a Test series starts. Although I give every English first-class cricketer a form to complete when he begins his career, it is not always easy to persuade touring players from overseas to complete them legibly. The Indians are inevitably the most polite, friendly and co-operative of visitors and the manager allowed me to measure Sunil and 'Vishy' in their dressing room at Old Trafford. Both removed their boots and stood with their backs against the wall. Their colleagues crowded round as I used my tape measure on them. 'Gavaskar 5ft 4¾in – Viswanath 5ft 4½in', I announced.

A great cheer went up but 'Vishy' demanded a recount!

When I began scoring for the BBC in 1966 I had very little data on the players that was not readily available to every cricket follower in the form of *Playfair Cricket Annual.* In those days we used to broadcast county championship matches for the various regions and World Service, and I visited all the counties during that season. When I discovered that G. E. Barker of Essex was just Gordon with no second name, I started checking all the others and my 'Newcomers' form was born. Not all newcomers were eager to reveal their full names. Those with names best concealed were John Darling Inchmore, the beefy Worcestershire seam bowler and big-hitting batsman, and John Devereaux Dubricious Pember (Leicestershire 1968/71) a robust rugby-playing farmer who had been inflicted with ancient family names at the behest of two wealthy maiden aunts.

Although few have concealed their names, many have been less than truthful about their ages. The true birth date of Basil D'Oliveira remained shrouded in mystery from everyone – including the Passport Office – for many seasons. Although no one believed that 4 October 1934 was correct, we could not disprove it. Eventually my enquiries to Cape Town bore fruit and the late Denys Heesom, the most thorough and competent of statisticians, sent me a copy of his birth certificate. It revealed that 'Dolly' had offloaded exactly three years of his early life.

D'Oliveira is far from being unique in hiding his age – although three years is slightly excessive. Before the last War it had been common practice for young professionals to engage in such forward planning in order to extend their careers. Nowadays birth certificates are usually required when a player is registered and such documents are readily accessible to the researching statistician. Only the Pakistanis remain immune and their ages are usually listed as 'unconfirmed'.

Brian Johnston was chiefly instrumental in my adding 'Height' to my Newcomers Form. John Arlott was amused by the idea of my wandering around dressing rooms with a tape measure. When I used to score the Sunday League for television, I had cards for each player and a frame to hold those of the four who were batting and bowling. On one memorable occasion, John noticed that all four were 6ft 3in tall. 'Ah!', he growled, 'All cricketers are 6ft 3in in Bill Frindall's book!'

I rely on fellow enthusiasts in each of the overseas countries playing first-class cricket to supply me with accurate scores of their matches and details of players I have not met. Without exception they are most helpful and devoted to what in most cases is their hobby and not their profession. I am extremely lucky in having a hobby that has got out of control. I reciprocate by helping them and in the last few years have had the great pleasure of visiting several of them for the first time after a postal relationship lasting up to 18 years.

As far as scores of matches in Britain are concerned, I am supplied with the official completed scorecards which each county (and Oxford and Cambridge Universities), issue after all its home matches. If there are discrepancies with the press version then I ask the official scorers for confirmation. Mistakes are bound to creep in but they have been greatly minimised in the last two decades, and particularly since the now 1,000-strong Association of Cricket Statisticians was formed.

For each match I have the career files of the 22 players taking part. These are looseleaf, foolscap forms which contain the manuscript details of every first-class match played by each player. A separate section extracts his Test match performances in great detail. More general records are covered by the *Test Cricket* and *Records* volumes which I compiled and edited for the Queen Anne Press Wisden Library. Both have been kept up to date on blank interleaves. I also have with me several other publications depending on the type of match we are broadcasting, and a good many files of notes and other relevant papers. Other documents and books are kept in my car which, by kindness of the ground authorities, is parked as close as possible to our boxes.

Fortunately I have been able to collect a fairly comprehensive library of cricket reference books which has gradually spread into three rooms of my flat. I live only seven miles from Lord's, with its magnificent library supervised by the ever-helpful Stephen Green, its curator. Equally close is the Newspaper Library at Colindale.

Many of the commentators' questions can be answered from my special scoring sheets, full details of which appeared in the first edition of 'Test Match Special'. On two occasions my method enabled me to restore runs for England that had been missed by the official scorers. Both were no-balls and both instances were clearly recalled by the umpires and players involved so that the scorers were instructed to correct their records. After the first one – at Edgbaston in 1978 – 'Dickie' Bird marched me into the England dressing room and told Mike Brearley that England's score had been increased by one run. 'Frindall's just scored his first run for England!', announced Mike to ribald cheers.

One item in my portable library has nothing whatsoever to do with cricket commentaries and is the result of Henry Blofeld's interest in just about everything that can be seen from our box that is totally unrelated to the play. It is 'The Complete Guide to British Wildlife' and was donated by its illustrator, Norman Arlott (no relation to John). Sorry, Henry!

B.J.'s SEVENTIETH

—————— Christopher Martin-Jenkins ——————

Now of my three score years and ten,
Seventy will not come again.

For some, that thought, with apologies to Houseman, might be an occasion for mourning. Not for Brian Johnston. We all celebrated his seventieth birthday as joyfully as if it had been his christening, and well we might have done, for there was not the slightest sign that his eternal boyhood was coming to an end. Because his birthday is in June there is a good chance that it will coincide with a Test match. Usually, indeed, it is the Lord's Test, and Brian and his wife Pauline often give a party for friends to celebrate. In 1982, it happened that the Test which coincided with his seventieth birthday was taking place instead at Old Trafford. Something had to be done, and it was.

The hotel where many of the commentators stay each year, the Swan at Bucklow Hill, started the day with a champagne breakfast in his honour. The commentators present were, as always, living examples of moderation in all things and the subsequent commentaries did not seem to suffer from the Bacchanalian start to the day. Those, however, who abhor mentions of cream cakes during cricket matches had a bad day because such was the quantity of cakes, sweets and other mainly edible gifts arriving at the commentary box through the rest of the day, that it was almost impossible not to refer to them occasionally. The England team, no doubt, at the instigation of their captain, an old friend of B.J.'s, presented him with a magnificent Stilton cheese. Generously he gave us all a large slice to take home with us.

In the evening the BBC gave a dinner in Brian's honour at New Broadcasting House in Manchester, to which we were all invited. During the drinks before the meal, and quite unaware that before the year was out Eamonn Andrews would be doing his own *This Is Your Life* programme on Brian, Peter Baxter and I surprised him with our own version of his life. My Eamonn Andrews accent is not up to Yarwood standard, but my script is given below and you should try to read it in an Andrews accent if you can! Peter collected the voices of several friends and members of the family on a tape recorder and Pauline, plus other members of the Johnston clan, appeared unexpectedly from behind a screen in a reasonable simulation of the real thing. Indeed Brian was so touched by her sudden appearance that he suddenly had to blow his nose several times with his handkerchief. (What else would he blow it with!)

CMJ's Script

CMJ (as Eamonn Andrews)   You thought this was just a private party, and so it is. But it's something else too, because tonight, Brian Alexander Johnston, wit, raconteur, bon viveur, bon appetit – This Is Your Life.

TAPE – THIS IS YOUR LIFE SIGNATURE TUNE (during which BJ is led to a strategically placed chair)

CMJ   You were born seventy years ago this very day at the Old Rectory, Little Berkhamsted, amidst the leafy lanes of rural Hertfordshire. (Pause for nausea at the flowery script)
Your father was a well-to-do coffee merchant and you were the fourth and most loquacious member of the family. The gift of the gab was to bring you much fame and even, when you retired from the BBC a little fortune. But you never had greater fortune than the day you met this fair lady.

TAPE – PAULINE JOHNSTON – What a fantastic birthday you're having – starting with champers at breakfast and all those celebrations in the box. I only wish I could be with you. Have a happy birthday, darling (can I say darling?) – and please keep me a slice from *one* of your cakes!

CMJ   The voice of your wife, Pauline, and tonight all the way from London, England, she has come here to be with you. Come in Pauline Johnston . . .
(Enter Pauline to B.J.'s amazement. Now he understands why his favourite room at the hotel had been mysteriously changed for a double.)

CMJ   As everyone who has read your six autobiographies knows well, you and Pauline have produced and directed five delightful children and here, by the magic of modern technology is the voice of each and every one of them.

TAPE – BARRY   (from Hollywood, where he was on a broadcasting course)

CLARE   (about to produce the first Johnston grandchild)

IAN   (with a self-made trumpet fanfare like one of his father's)

JOANNA   (with a chorus of 'Happy Birthday to You')

ANDREW   (from Sydney, where he is in publishing)

CMJ   Well, for Andrew there and one or two others, even the enormous *This Is Your Life* budget was not enough, but two of your youngsters have travelled to Manchester to be with you tonight. Come in Clare and husband David.
(Enter Clare and David)

CMJ   So now restored to the family of your bosom, we journey back to your youth. Your old nanny, Nanny Harding, later to become famous as Gilbert Harding, remembers you well.

TAPE – NANNY HARDING (a totally fictitious being, like many to come, portrayed by Peter Baxter). He was always such a noisy little boy. He never would stop talking or making a noise like a trumpet!

CMJ   Your parents, tired of your constant corny jokes, sent you to school in Eastbourne where the headmaster, Bugs Waterfield, taught you the facts of life and also recorded this message before being called to the great headmaster's study in the sky.

TAPE – BUGS WATERFIELD (one of the many voices of CMJ). Johnston was what I would call a silly boy – silly but lovable – no malice in the boy, nothing a good caning couldn't put right. He was also, in my humble opinion, the finest exponent behind the timbers since Gregor McGregor.

CMJ   At Eton your interest in cricket grew and amongst other distinctions you became a member of Pop. You've been one ever since. No broadcaster (with the possible exception of Eamonn Andrews) has ever been so popular.
You had a distinguished war, liberating Belgium single-handed and even winning the grudging admiration of Regimental Sergeant Major Upcock.

TAPE – R.S.M. UPCOCK (Peter Baxter). Hoh, yes, Mistah Johnston was a very fine hofficer. Very difficult to keep his mind on military matters, of course, but worth his weight in gold when the bugler was on sick parade!

'Brian Johnston, This is Your Life' – the real thing.

CMJ   You joined the BBC and swiftly made a name for yourself as an entertainer of great versatility. But cricket was your great love and you were soon touring the world with England teams, sometimes finding players who were equally attracted to the business of show business.

TAPE – COLIN MILBURN (Singing 'Underneath the Arches' – which used to be his double act with BJ on tour. He breaks off).
It's no good, I can't do it without Johnners on the piano.

CMJ   Your old friend and singing companion, Ollie Flanagan Milburn. Just one of many commentators to wish you great happiness on this, we hope, joyful evening.

TAPE – MESSAGES FROM: TREVOR BAILEY (admiring an innings which occupied seventy years)
FRED TRUEMAN (deploring the state of BJ's suits)
DON MOSEY (raising the question of the acceptability of 'CLYST' in their word game)
CMJ (thanking BJ for his kindness to this particular schoolboy many years ago)
HENRY BLOFELD (recalling some of BJ's less repeatable gaffes)
TONY LEWIS (asking why he is singled out to be called by his initials – Arl)
PETER BAXTER (suggesting more rehearsal is needed for the close of play highlights summary)
BILL FRINDALL (recalling an incident at Southend when BJ paralysed him by standing on his headphone cable and then read out the note which said, 'please raise your left foot')
THE NAWAB OF PATAUDI (recalling Ajit Wadekar's loss of the command of English when approached by BJ for a live interview)

CMJ   Many of your friends are here tonight. Many more are thinking of you including this absent friend in South Africa.

TAPE – RICHARD MADDOCK (former TMS producer who retired from his post in the BBC's Midland region in 1981)

CMJ   And from a fine BBC voice to an equally fine ABC voice.

TAPE – ALAN McGILVRAY   You know he's always caught me with a piece of cake in my mouth – and he's done that purposely sometimes. But it's been very good fun and I know he'll enjoy this. When you called me to record this, I was preparing my dinner and putting some frozen peas into a container. I had a whisky beside it and I poured the peas into the whisky!
I'd like to be able to give him a pair of tan and white shoes – he seems to like those.

CMJ   One voice remains. A voice as familiar and warm as your own. All the way from the English Channel, come in the Duke of Alderney.

TAPE – JOHN ARLOTT   Oh gentlemen – assuming that you're up to your usual nasty tricks and no ladies are present – and especially you Bjorn Bjornston, good luck to you all. I hear, Bjorn, that you're now 95; I thought it was only 85. Anyway I hope that you've had a good day and that the Alderman has fixed the weather – it's rained all day – you've had no play – he's beaten you at the word game (I wonder what would happen if you two ever met someone who could spell?) – and that you're so crammed with liquorice allsorts that you've barely got room for your Pouilly Fumée.
I do still listen to you sometimes, so plough on my boys – booze till all hours and a very happy birthday, Bjorn.

CMJ   All of us join John Arlott in wishing you many, many happy returns and expressing the hope that one day Eamonn Andrews really will say, 'Brian Johnston, THIS IS YOUR LIFE.'

POST SCRIPT

Sure enough, he did.

Before the season was out we were being summoned to Lord's, under conditions of top secrecy, to record a few spoofs for the real programme.

The programme itself was a tremendously enjoyable experience for all concerned, especially, of course, for the man whose life we were celebrating. I think even the people who compile and produce the programme felt that there was something special about this one. I hope, if Eamonn is still with us – or we are still with Eamonn! – they will do another programme on Brian's life when he reaches 100!

THE COUNTY CIRCUIT
— Henry Blofeld —

There cannot be a much more enjoyable pursuit than spending the summer watching County cricket around England. It may not be as glamorous a way of life as travelling round the world following Test cricket, but it has a delightful, unhurried charm all of its own.

Even today with the motorways, the long list of overseas players and a heavy programme of one-day cricket, the counties still have their own innate characteristics on the cricket field. Indeed, players like Mike Procter and Clive Lloyd who have come from overseas have even managed to pick up the essential flavour of their adopted homes.

But I believe strongly that writing and broadcasting about cricket involves so much more than simply watching two teams in action in the middle. There are the grounds I visit, the hotels in which I stay, the people I meet and sometimes stay with, the journeys I make, the restaurants in which I eat, the exceptional bottle of claret, the bores and a host of other things all of which go to make up an English summer.

They all help to shape my life in England between, say, 20 April and 14 September. I think they help too, perhaps, to put the game of cricket into the necessary perspective of its environment and, most important of all, they provide me with so much fun.

In May 1983, I went down to Taunton to watch Somerset play a one-day John Player League match against Essex on the Sunday, and then to finish off their three-day Championship match on the Monday and Tuesday. My adventures over the three days just about encapsulated the joy I find in travelling the county circuit.

My journey began one Sunday morning before the start of the World Cup at Paddington Station when I discovered that my British Rail timetable was out of date, but mercifully the train left later than I had anticipated. It left at 11.45 and not 11.25 and still arrived in Taunton at 2.11.

For once the ticket queue was short and armed with a mountain of Sunday papers, I settled down for the journey. A pale sun had been shining in London, but the further west we went the darker it became and sometime before we arrived it began to pour which it had apparently been doing since five o'clock in the morning.

The ticket collector at the station told me the match was off, and I waited half an hour before I got a taxi to take me to the Castle Hotel. It is one of my favourite hotels on the circuit and I have stayed there for years.

There is a charming country town atmosphere in Taunton which comes through strongly even in the back of a taxi on a wet Sunday afternoon. We negotiated the one-way system and there was The Castle across the car park from the Winchester Arms. The wisteria over the front of the hotel was in full flower and the entrance with the familiar smiling porter had that friendly feel.

I had a delightful room looking out over the quiet side and I found a small bottle of Amontillado sherry with a card from David Prior, the manager. The wet afternoon gave me the chance to catch up on a few of those one-off articles which I always leave to the last possible moment. At the time I was on fairly strict diet to lose weight after an overindulgent tour of Australia and I stuck to my typewriter until half past seven before sneaking down to the bar.

Before I came down I rang up Gerald Pawle, and old friend who lives in Penzance and has for years covered cricket predominantly in the west country for the *Daily Telegraph*. I had half expected to find him at The Castle, but he now told me that he had decided to stop reporting cricket and was involved in writing a book about the former England captain, Bob Wyatt, who also lives in Cornwall.

After a glass of wine I went back to my room to watch the first in the repeat of the television series 'Yes Minister'. It was almost nine o'clock when I arrived in the restaurant and the first person I saw as I came through the door sitting at a table by himself was Martin Wood.

He is a second-hand book dealer who is especially interested in cricket books and lives in Kent and is a fairly constant figure on English grounds particularly on the big occasions. I joined him and heard all about his latest acquisitions and before the night was out he had lent me a book of cricket songs published in the 1890s.

I cannot have been sitting at his table for more than five minutes when I suddenly saw at a table across the room two old friends, Maurice and Elaine Berkeley. They are passionate Essex supporters and go everywhere to watch the county, but the previous week I had spent five days in Chelmsford watching Essex and had not seen them.

Maurice told me he had just reached 80 which was a surprise for he looks younger. Elaine had not been too well in the winter and during the wet

weather of May they had decided to stay at home. Normally, they go to all Essex's away matches but this year they admitted that they were going to give Cardiff and Old Trafford a miss.

Somehow Essex matches are not complete without Maurice and Elaine and the game of cricket has few stauncher supporters although both can be strongly critical at times and usually our likes and dislikes coincide. Unlike many supporters of the game they are keenly appreciative of the technical side of it all, too.

They had driven to Taunton on the Friday and on the Saturday night had had Keith Fletcher and David Acfield to dinner and Graham Gooch and Keith Pont had been selected for the Monday night. I promised to sit with them at the cricket the following day and to tell them about the Australian tour.

On the Monday before, Essex in the persons of Norbert Phillip and Neil Foster, had bowled out Surrey in 64 minutes for fourteen and after the game had ended I had collected a couple of scorecards to keep. Martin Wood soon put me in my place over this when he told me that he had ordered a hundred and they had been brought down to Taunton for him.

He tried to persuade me to play a game of chess with him after dinner, a game which I have never understood and so he went off to the bar where he had located an Essex supporter who did.

The next day my early morning tea was delivered sharply at seven o'clock and my curtains were pulled revealing a lovely sunny day. It is difficult to fault The Castle, but the price of a cooked breakfast was £5.20 which I thought was a little steep for a boiled egg and a piece of toast.

But just across the road by the front door is a small cafe which serves breakfast. Feeling slightly traitorous, I decided that this was the answer. For some reason boiled eggs were beyond them but the poached egg on toast and coffee was excellent for 77p even if a trifle too calorific. I hope my employers appreciate these small savings.

On my walk down to the ground I bought my picnic lunch at the County Stores in the High Street and then turned right into James Street past the church and the pub delightfully called 'The Ring of Bells'. When I climbed the staircase to the press box I found that the only person there sitting in his inner sanctum surrounded by telephones was Eric Hill.

Cricket in Somerset is unthinkable without Eric. As a freelance journalist he has covered Somerset cricket since his playing days with the county ended in the fifties and no-one is more helpful or friendly in any English press box. He told me all about the troubles Somerset had had during the winter when the committee had wanted to dispense with the services of Peter McCombe who looks after the lives of Ian Botham and Viv Richards. When it became an issue, England were playing Northern New South Wales in Newcastle where I had to interview Botham about it all for he and Richards had threatened to leave Somerset if McCombe was kicked out.

Eric's pungent comments are always well worth listening to and he filled me in with all the gossip over the appointment of Tony Brown as Somerset's new secretary. Brown had captained Gloucestershire and then taken over as secretary there when Graham Parker retired. We also talked about New Zealand beer with which Eric struck up a particularly close relationship when covering one England tour there.

The Taunton press box is old and rickety but quite delightful and is part of the charm of the ground. There's not much room and soon Mike Austin of the *Daily Telegraph,* Peter Jackson of the *Daily Mail* and John Davies of the *Daily Express* were cooped up inside. I had not seen any of them since the previous summer and so there was plenty of catching up to do.

It was a gentle day's cricket when not much happened for a long time until Ian Botham hit 34 off 16 balls in fourteen minutes hitting two sixes and four fours. Then it was back to watching the slumbering progress of Peter Roebuck.

After a time I walked round past the old pavilion to the Stragglers Bar to see if Alan Gibson might be there for I had had an idea that he might have been covering the match for *The Times.* I could not find him, but I located Maurice and Elaine in the stand on the other side of the old pavilion and we had a splendid hour together.

While we were talking I spotted Alan Gibson walking round to the Stragglers Bar. Soon, I followed him for there is no one more entertaining to watch a day's cricket with than Alan. His delightful reports in *The Times* may not always conform to the accepted norm for these things, but they are always the greatest of fun as he describes his adventures while travelling to the ground – British Rail always comes in for a good deal of stick – and he also talks of those he meets while watching the game. I never miss one of his pieces and they should be compulsory reading.

He told me that he had been sixty a fortnight before and I so well remembered him celebrating his fiftieth birthday on the Taunton ground for he began his piece the next day by saying, 'I reached my half century yesterday which was more than any batsman on either side.' During our conversation we moaned about the rigorous travelling programme watching the World Cup would entail and generally had a good old gossip and a pleasant drink in the sun.

I was warmly greeted by Herbert Hoskins a former chairman of Somerset whom I had last seen during the First Test Match in Perth in November. It was sad that the noise and good cheer that invariably comes from the old Somerset cricketer, Bill Andrews was absent but sadly he was unwell and was confined to barracks in Weston-super-Mare.

Altogether it was a marvellously enjoyable day which finished with the walk back up the High Street to the Castle Hotel. In the bar before dinner I talked to Graham Gooch and Keith Pont who were Maurice and Elaine's guests for dinner. Then, after an excellent dinner, I slipped away to finish Douglas Jardine's book about the Bodyline tour, *In Quest of the Ashes.*

The next morning was grey and cloudy and as always on a third day I hoped that I might have a bit of luck and be able to catch an early train back to London. The Somerset batsmen were obliging because they collapsed against the off-break bowling of David Acfield whom I always love to see take wickets, for he is one of the most delightful and amusing of all county cricketers. He and Ray East form a marvellous double act in the Essex dressing room. Their take-off of Trevor Bailey writing a piece for the *Financial Times* in the Essex dressing room while still captain of the county and receiving reports on progress from the middle from a player by the window is hysterical.

I caught the early train easily and arrived back in London in time for dinner with Anna and a solicitor friend. They had been three days which had for me been a perfect illustration of the charm of county cricket and my luck in having such a wonderful job. It might have been the George and Dragon at Fordwich just outside Canterbury, the Peacock at Rowsley which is convenient for Chesterfield, Sheffield and Worksop, the Swan at Bucklow Hill for Old Trafford, The Francis at Bath, The Cottage-in-the-Wood in Malvern for Worcester and countless others.

Or I might have been staying with Geoffrey and Clarissa Palmer at Carlton Curlieu for a Leicestershire match when I would almost certainly have been drinking copious quantities of Geoffrey's impeccable claret. They are all important signposts in the intriguing, compelling and delightful way of life which comes from watching county cricket in England.

OUR SATURDAY GUESTS
Brian Johnston

For me the most pleasant duty during a Test Match is the twenty minute interview spot every Saturday lunchtime. We invite well-known personalities from all walks of life to come and chat to us about themselves and, of course, cricket. The only qualification which they need is a love of cricket. If the guest can or has played, so much the better. But otherwise watching it, reading about it or merely following it in the papers is sufficient. Inevitably the close association of cricket and the arts means that most of our guests are actors, writers, singers and so on. I would also like to have said actresses, but alas we missed the opportunity of asking Celia Johnson and Gladys Henson – two great cricket watchers and enthusiasts.

In the First Test at Lord's against India in 1982 Brian Rix revealed that he first played cricket when aged three, and that he went on to play for Hull in the East Yorkshire League. His fast-medium bowling flourished more than his batting, because he was three years in the League before he discovered that he was short-sighted. But at least he once made fifty at Lord's for the Lord's Taverners against Old England.

He used to open the bowling for the Stage with Bill Franklyn, whose father Leo played in all Brian's farces and once uttered the memorable line: 'There are fairies at the garden of my bottom!'

Brian declared himself a disenfranchised Yorkshireman, because officially there is no longer an East Riding. Jimmy Binks is the only Yorkshire cricketer from that area, but there must be something in the air which breeds actors. Tom Courtenay, John Alderton, Ian Carmichael and Dickie Henderson all come from there.

Brian served in the RAF during the war and had the distinction of being turned out of a net at Harrogate by a certain Squadron Leader L. E. G. Ames, who happened to want a bit of practice. Incidentally, Brian told us that, although he had played farce at either the Whitehall or Garrick for thirty years, he always refused to act the fool when playing in charity matches. Goodness knows how many times he lost his trousers on the stage during those thirty years, but although frequently asked to do so out in the middle at cricket, he never did. He has now 'kindly left the stage' to become Secretary-General of that admirable charity for the mentally handicapped, Mencap, and he proudly boasted that only 8% of the donations is spent on administration.

In the Third Test against India at the Oval it was the turn of that astronomer, xylophonist, and cricketer extraordinary, Patrick Moore. He plays his cricket for Selsey and his ambition when he was with us on July 18th was to make his first run of the season. In the previous year he had only achieved this feat in September! But he bowls medium-pace spin and takes a run of fourteen yards – not unlike that of Doug Wright – which has been described as 'a kangaroo doing a barn dance'.

Among his cricketing achievements was playing at the Oval for the RAF, and on another occasion being caught by an umpire and given out! But his most remarkable game of cricket was undoubtedly one played in the restaurant of the Russell Hotel. Patrick used a long French loaf as a bat, Pat Pocock bowled a roll, and the stumps were the legs of an Italian waiter with his trousers rolled up.

We naturally asked Patrick about the possibility of cricket on the Moon. He thought that the surface – though dusty – would be fairly firm, if a bit bumpy. Two things worried him. As the Moon's gravity is only one-sixteenth of that of the Earth, Ian Botham when running up to bowl might suddenly go into orbit. And if cricket spread into outer space, how on earth would M.C.C. evolve an L.B.W. law for three-legged Martians!

I suppose the most hilarious View from the Boundary in 1982 was when our guests at Lord's were Peter Tinniswood, author of Tales from the Long Room, and More Tales from the Long Room, and Robin Bailey, who – as the Brigadier – has immortalised the Tales on TV, radio and record.

Tinners – as I call him – is 100% Lancashire, with boyhood memories of Makepeace and Hallows, and with Winston Place as his undying hero. He did not play much cricket. He was small and frightened of a cricket ball. Robin admitted he had only once reached double figures, but regarded cricket as a fantasy, and watched it whenever he could.

Tinners explained that he wrote the Long Room books because he thought that most cricket humour was anecdotal, and he wanted to write some creative humour. So he created the Brigadier – born in Arlott St John and now resident in Witney Scrotum. He had watched Robin as Uncle Mort in the TV series *I Didn't Know You Cared*, and based his Brigadier on Robin's deep voice and military bearing. He also created a number of fantasy names: E. W. (Gloria) Swanton, E. R. Elizabeth Regina Dexter, Rev. Don Mosey Moderator of the Free Church of Lancashire, and Lord Henry Blofeld

Three of our Saturday guests: Henry Kelly, Patrick Moore and Brian Rix.

from Blofeld Revisited, whose father the 10th Duke of Wisden was involved in the 1922 abdication crisis with Mrs Simpson, mother of Bobby Simpson, Captain of Australia!

He went on to tell us some of his cricket recipes.

Arlott Cake:
 A rich fruity concoction, aromatic and deeply satisfying to the soul. A cake to eat with vintage port.

Swanton Pudding:
 A heavy suet-based confectionary, which he found intimidating and indigestible and turned the custard lumpy.

Auntie Lewis's Welsh Tart:
 An over-fussy dessert.

Jonners Jam Sandwich
 A jolly cake full of fun and hearty flavour. Marvellous for tuck boxes and midnight feasts in the dorm.

We pointed out to him his obvious fetish for Alec Bedser and his twin brother Eric, who feature prominently in the books. So we asked Robin to read us a piece in which the Twins were mentioned. He chose a postcard which Peter had sent him when on holiday in Canada during a trip across the Rockies by train. It read: 'Arrived here Tuesday. Super four-day train ride. I opened the innings for passengers against the crew, and was doing well until derailed at Winnipeg for 32. The Bedser Twins send their regards. They are on the M.C.C. engine-spotting tour of North America.'

And so it went on, and I must admit that the cricket after lunch compared unfavourably with the fantasy world of Peter and the Brigadier.

In the final Test of the season at Headingley against Pakistan, singer/entertainer, TV and radio star Ian Wallace climbed up to our box in the Rugby stand. It was obviously going to be a musical session. Don Mosey was with me and he and Ian were soon singing the Judge's song from Trial by Jury. When we were able to talk Ian told us that his cricket started at Charterhouse where he had once made ninety-nine for a team called 2nd Tics when his captain somewhat unkindly declared. He is a member of M.C.C., supports Middlesex and just likes watching. He says he was born in Middlesex to save the fare.

He has done everything from opera at La Scala to pantomime at the Leeds Empire. In fact he played the Sheriff of Nottingham in the last-ever performance at that theatre. Some of the audience staged a sit-in in protest at the closure. As the manager said to Ian: 'If only they'd put bums on seats a bit earlier they wouldn't be pulling the theatre down now'.

Throughout his career Ian has been asked for his famous Hippopotamus song. In fact his autobiography is called *Please Sing Something About Mud.* So the Headingley spectators in the Rugby stand were soon regaled with 'Mud, mud, glorious mud', Ian and Don Mosey supplying the vocals, whilst I did my rather poor imitation of a trombone accompaniment. Ian concluded proceedings by singing a delightful cricket song called 'The Cricketers of Hambledon' by Peter Warlock and Bruce Blunt, and he just managed to finish it as the umpires came out at the end of the lunch interval.

As I write this, the 1983 Oval Test has just finished. On the Saturday our guests were Richard Stilgoe and Peter Skellern – both wildly enthusiastic about cricket, with Peter Skellern, in spite of the risk of injury involved, being a wicket-keeper. And on seeing the size of his hands they did seem to suit wicket-keeping rather than piano-playing.

Again, inevitably, we had plenty of music, and our tour de force was a rendering of 'The Way you Look Tonight', with Peter Skellern doing trumpet and vocals, Richard Stilgoe percussion, myself the usual trombone, and Jenkers on banjo. Alan Curtis, who does the P.A. at the Tests, recorded it and then to the astonishment of the crowd, played it over the public address system. I *have* heard worse bands – but not many!

But I suppose our most remarkable recording at that Oval Test was when we visited Dickie Bird in the umpires' room before the game. He was bemoaning the fact that he had just bought a cottage and was woken every morning at 5.30am by the peacocks of the previous owners. He then proceeded to give an imitation of a peacock's cry, which would have made Percy Edwards jealous. We rushed to get a tape recorder and Dickie kindly repeated his raucous cry. We played it over the air during a stoppage of play, and again during the lunch interval. It must be *the* quiz question for the winter season: 'Name a Bird – not a peacock – which makes a peacock's cry'.

THE BAXTER DIARY IN AUSTRALIA 1982/3

Peter Baxter

Friday 5 November

Colder than I expected – puddles on the ground, but at 5 a.m. in Perth I am not too inclined to pass comment on Australia, especially not after a 21 hour flight which had started with a four hour delay due to industrial action. My first impression of the great island continent is helped by my taxi driver – a 'New Australian' only six years out from Germany.

Bed was the first priority, and after an eight hour sleep, interrupted only by a call from Henry Blofeld to enquire after both my presence and health.

When I rose it was to pay my first call to the Australian Broadcasting Commission only a few doors away, a building which had been part of my taxi driver's guided tour the night before. This was to be a tour of coming face to face with familiar names I had dealt with from 12,000 miles away, and the first of these, ABC's sports producer in Western Australia, George Grjlusich, was very helpful and friendly to start me off. He took me to the WACA ground where the England match against the State side had started that morning and where the inevitable cries of 'What sort of time do you call this?' greeted me from the press box.

I was shown the box which had been set aside for our commentary on the Test Match which was to start a week today. It was a pleasant-looking ground, not over-endowed with grandstand seating but surrounded by the traditional Australian grassy banks referred to everywhere – not just Sydney – as 'hills'. My first encounter with the hill wit came as I walked round the ground when Norman Cowans was in the process of bundling Western Australia out for 167. As he ran in I heard the cry 'The only good Pom is a black Pom!'

Henry's splendidly old-fashioned club, The Weld, gave me not only a delightful first evening in Australia, but also my first taste of what could easily become addictive – Australian steak.

Saturday 6 November

Waking, refreshed, at 5.30 a.m. suggested that jet lag was not completely shaken off, but at least it did not feel too bad.

The previous day Norman Cowans had had a hand in dismissing Western Australia for 167, but Dennis Lillee had shown that it might not be such a bad score as he and Alderman removed Tavaré and Gower on that first evening. So it was to prove as England struggled with the exception of Ian Botham, riding his luck for 65. Little did we imagine that this was to be his highest score of the tour. England's first innings ended with them 11 runs behind, and by the close that deficit had widened to 124 with only three Western Australian wickets down.

Henry Blofeld and I were together in the ABC box at the close of play as he delivered what must have been more than his thousandth report of the tour and I broke my duck.

Sunday 7 November

The weather was warming up steadily to the point I had expected of Australia. England's bowlers chipped their way efficiently enough through Western Australia, but still were set 209 to win and made a disastrous start, losing two wickets for 7 and 5 for 82, but Derek Randall kept them in the hunt leaving 41 needed for victory at the close.

Monday 8 November

The game finished in an hour in the morning, but not without giving any England sympathisers present heart-failure. England did win, though, by one wicket after getting past 200 with only 6 wickets down. Derek Randall won his first, but, we suspected, not his last battle with Lillee making 92.

With the greatly increased workload of a weekday after being broken in gently at the week end, I was glad of the early finish giving me the chance to script my reports in leisurely fashion and interview Randall to send it all back by telephone from the comfort of my hotel room.

Tuesday 9 November

An early call from the *Daily Telegraph* correspondent, Michael Carey, suggested the hiring of a car to see something of the countryside outside Perth. So, with Matthew Engel of the *Guardian,* away we went up the coast road north out of Perth past sand dunes and magnificent, tempting beaches until we were free of the sprawling suburbs. One futuristic holiday village offered us the delights of a dolphinarium and just up the road we were able to get close to koalas and kangaroos and be laughed at by kookaburras. For the rest, our excursion gave me a first tiny idea of the size of Australia as mile after mile of straight road bordered by nothing but the occasional eucalyptus unfolded before us. Looking at the map I realised how little of the island continent we had actually seen on a day's drive.

Wednesday 10 November

The event of the day was to be a lunch given by the sponsors to launch the Test series. Ironically it came on the State's declared 'smoke free day' when everyone had been exhorted to give up the dreaded weed. One man, would, I was sure, remain faithful to the sponsors. Sure enough, I found Alan McGilvray under a halo of smoke supporting our hosts – Benson and Hedges.

Thursday 11 November

The eve of a Test series is always a busy day and this one started with a working breakfast for the England press party at which PBL Marketing expounded their promotional activities on behalf of the Australian Cricket Board. We were shown video recordings of the TV commercials as well as posters and other material. I found it rather chilling and felt uneasy about the abrasive style of it and the rabble-rousing nature of the commercials not to say despairing at the implied need for it. Surely the Ashes, the greatest of all cricket contests did not need selling like this? Somehow the subtleties of cricket seemed to be submerged in a plethora of 'concepts' and promises of furious action, which might, or might not, be lived up to. Money seemed to figure all too largely in most of the addresses to us.

The timing of the team announcement enabled me to have a fresh story for the early morning news programmes back home where they were eight hours behind Perth. Five reports needed telephoning and then more had to be written for the evening satellite circuit to London from the ABC studios next door.

We now interrupt the Baxter Diary for a report on the First Test by Henry Blofeld . . .

THE FIRST TEST
PERTH – England get the draw. *HENRY BLOFELD.*

The first morning of a Test series is a tense occasion for everyone involved, especially when England is playing Australia: players, officials, journalists, commentators, selectors and even for spectators now that we seem to live in an age where non-partisan spectatorship is a thing of the past.

I am sure that all of us in the commentary box or the press box do our level best to be impartial and simply to enjoy the cricket. But when the Ashes are at stake, it is mighty difficult.

I arrived early at the ground of the Western Australian Cricket Association in Perth, the WACA, which has more the atmosphere of a country town ground than a main Test centre. It was already filling up nicely with long queues at all the gates although the limit is not much more than 20,000.

It is just as important, to us at any rate, for Test Match Special to get the series off to a good start as it is for the two sides. Our commentary point at the WACA was an open desk with room for three people in the front of a small open air box just below the megaton Channel Nine Television box just alongside the press box.

Peter Baxter was already there hurrying about making sure that everything was just so. The Bearded Wonder, Bill Frindall, was, as always, another early arrival and he had set up his camp in the far corner of the desk, but now the first problem occurred.

This same box was also the point from where the local commercial radio station 6PR, kept their listeners informed of the day's events with frequent crossovers for short reports. As luck would have it, I was doing all 6PR's reports, but the station was in danger of being squeezed out by the BBC.

All was well in the end, because I agreed to sit on the raised step just behind the commentary desk and to do my reports down the line from there. I was also working for commercial stations in the other main Australian cities and every hour I had to go across to my seat in the press box where Radio 2UE in Sydney had installed a telephone for my use.

It all kept me fairly busy and on the whole tour of Australia and New Zealand I managed to get through just over 4,000 separate broadcasts. It kept me fit, too, for I was for ever running like a mountain goat from one point to the next and back again, knocking people over as I went. In Adelaide and Melbourne it was quite a journey, too.

When I returned to England I was often told that my reports round Australia were distinctly audible over Radio 3. This was because of the close proximity of the different points I was operating from in Perth and Sydney.

On that first morning in Perth, Michael Carey was also an early arrival. It must have been a particularly tense moment for him as this was his first Test Match as a commentator. There was no need for him to worry, because he came through with flying colours.

I had not been there long before the always cheerful face of Peter Loader appeared. Peter had worked as a radio and television commentator for the Australian Broadcasting Commission, and also for Kerry Packer's Channel 9, and was as relaxed as he was experienced.

A resonant 'Hello Sunshine' announced the arrival of the ebullient Fred Trueman who did not stop at our box, but climbed further up the steps to the Channel 9 Emporium. He was, like me, wearing more than one hat.

I cannot remember when Chris Martin-Jenkins clocked in, but I expect it was only seconds before he was scheduled to go on the air. He likes to cut it fine and arrives with a look of complete bewilderment as to why anyone should be in the least worried. I am not sure how many of his now considerable and venerable number of grey hairs, Peter Baxter attributes to CMJ's timing, or lack of it!

The time difference between London and Perth at that time of the year is eight hours and in this First Test we did live commentary back home for the last four hours of the day. We had all been hoping that when the first moment came we would be able to give those listening in the middle of a cold winter some news to warm them up.

In the previous match, against Western Australia, Dennis Lillee had caused problems and was still obviously a bowler to be reckoned with. Poor Chris Tavaré had made a pair of spectacles against him in that game. When Greg Chappell won the toss, therefore, and put England in, England's supporters will have clenched their teeth and waited.

Geoff Cook and Chris Tavaré looked all too frail and insecure in the opening overs and when, at 14, Cook could only fend a lifter from Lillee to short-leg, I was not the only one who felt a sickening sense of déjà vu. It was Lillee's 329th Test wicket and at that moment it seemed to me that all 329 had been English opening batsmen. It was all so terrifyingly familiar. But then, Tavaré and David Gower batted with increasing confidence through to lunch when the score was 66–1.

Peter Baxter and I had spent the morning bumping into each other as he raced up the stairs to do his telephoned reports for BBC, and I was going at full speed in the other direction to look after the interests of either 6PR in Perth, 2UE in Sydney, 5DN in Adelaide, 4KQ in Brisbane, or 3UZ in Melbourne. In the middle of a broadcast I often used to forget who I was talking to.

Then, during the lunch interval, the great moment arrived when I heard Joanne Watson, our producer in London, hand over to me in

Perth. I was able to welcome listeners with the 'good news that England were 66–1 at lunch'. It is a marvellous moment, probably the most exciting of all for me, to start commentary on any day from abroad when, I always hope, people in their countless thousands are propped up in bed nervously sipping tea as they wait for the news. Perhaps in reality, it is only two long distance lorry drivers and the owner of an all-night hot-dog stall.

The afternoon's play began and there were no alarms as England built on their good start. Unfortunately both Gower and Allan Lamb got out just when a hundred seemed to be theirs for the asking. Ian Botham soon went to a hotly disputed catch behind off Geoff Lawson and, although we were not to know it then, this was the start of a desperate run with the bat which lasted right through the tour.

England were 242–4 at the end of the first day and on the second, thanks to Tavaré and Derek Randall, they finished with 411, which was pretty good for a side which had been put in to bat. Again we had good news for listeners at home, but sadly all that was forgotten late in the afternoon when in the middle of one of my commentary spells, we had a desperate outburst of hooliganism by drunken spectators which caused a fourteen-minute hold up and a nasty injury to Terry Alderman.

Bob Willis had just edged a drive against Alderman to the third-man boundary which brought up the 400. There was the usual applause and then from the public side of the ground by the scoreboard, several spectators wearing Union Jack tee-shirts jumped over the fence from the scoreboard side of the ground and ran out presumably to congratulate Willis.

Players have more and more taken the law into their own hands on these occasions and this happened again when the leading lout had reached the middle and after a quick dance had then begun his return journey. He passed close to Alderman who pushed him away whereupon he aimed a swing at the bowler which seemed to connect with his head and Alderman, in his fury, gave chase with Lillee and Allan Border behind, in close support.

They had almost reached the boundary rope when Alderman launched himself into a violent rugger tackle and felled his adversary. But in the process of falling, Alderman managed to dislocate his shoulder and pinch a nerve. He had to be carried off and took no further part in the entire season's cricket.

At the time, my mind went back to the riots which Don Mosey and I had described to listeners in Britain from Lahore in December 1977. I was on the air then too, when that one started. It began in high good humour as a ground invasion to congratulate Mudassar Nazar on reaching what eventually turned out to be the slowest hundred ever scored in Test cricket. It ended in disaster when a policeman took a lathi stick to a small boy and the crowd erupted. Mudassar had only reached 99 and the full story is in our first *Test Match Special* book.

This incident in Perth began in drunken humour and only turned sour when the players became involved. As we said at the time and Peter Loader and Fred Trueman who should know, were firm to stress, players should never get involved in these situations. One thing is sure, Alderman will not the next time.

At the end of the second day Australia were 30–0 in reply to England's 411 and the game was surely safe. The next day Greg Chappell scored yet another hundred and with John Dyson and Graeme Wood playing useful supporting roles, Australia reached 333–6.

They declared at 424–9 on the fourth day, 13 runs ahead, but England began their second innings badly and were suddenly in danger of defeat. Gower may have been unlucky to be lbw to Lillee, but Lamb gave his wicket away to Lawson who then bowled Botham for a duck. When the last day began England were 150 runs ahead with five wickets in hand and an Australian victory was very much on the cards.

On that last day, the anxious voices of the commentators must have reflected only too well each shift of the advantage as England fought hard not to lose a match they had already appeared to have saved. Randall, Bob Taylor, Derek Pringle and, most surprisingly, Norman Cowans at the end of the innings managed to keep Australia out.

Bill Frindall's calculator was working overtime to tell us the likely run rate that Australia would have to achieve if the remaining wickets fell, in ten minutes, in half an hour, 45 minutes and so on. Every run was crucial to England because it was another run Australia would then have to score.

Peter Loader was always supremely confident that England would save the day and so was Fred Trueman. I am afraid I was not nearly so faithful having watched England's batsmen over the years mess up situations which were considerably less dangerous than this one.

Anyway, England got their draw and we in the box felt that we had got a draw, too. I am sure some people hold commentators responsible for bad news and I was glad that there was no blame to attach this time. Mercifully, that evening we did not have the slightest idea of the indignities which lay ahead of England's cricketers.

Peter Baxter resumes his diary . . .

Thursday 18 November
After spending my first fortnight in Australia in Perth, I had mixed feelings about leaving it, but I was certainly keen to see more of the country and everyone else in the party had been raving to me about the splendours of Sydney. I was pleased with the way Test Match Special had started its series, and on the field the match had shown us two apparently even sides and the prospect of a sternly contested rubber. The first match of the series was important for teams on and off the field.

A four hour flight took us from the Indian Ocean coast straight across the country to the Pacific and a magnificent first view of Australia's first city. The Sydney Harbour Bridge and the Opera House look ridiculously like tourist souvenir models.

We arrived, after adding the three-hour time difference for crossing Australia, in early evening. I was immediately aware on the taxi drive to the hotel, of the faster pace of living here. This certainly was a city which did not go to sleep at 8.30 each night! Our hotel gave every indication of being able to give us a very comfortable stay and we had the nearby bustle and excitement of the King's Cross area, known to many as Sydney's red light district. There were plenty of eye opening sights!

Friday 19 November
Later in the afternoon I had my first sight of the Sydney Cricket Ground. The occasion was the launching of a book in the members' bar of the fine Victorian pavilion. Before I went in, I stood for a while at the boundary's edge and looked round the famous ground which had always seemed almost a figment of my imagination as I had listened to commentaries on cold winter mornings at home.

Then in the pavilion I met a man who exactly fifty years ago must have been a frightening prospect on this ground. Now a spry 78 year old great-grandfather living in Sydney, it was a great delight to meet and talk to Harold Larwood.

Saturday 20 November
It is sometimes hard for both players and media to keep their concentration for the state games once the Test series has started. Even so, this four day game against New South Wales was too important for some players trying to retain or gain a Test place to be dismissed lightly.

I was impressed immediately by the efficiency which had an official bringing my plug-in telephone up to the press box almost before I had discovered where I should be sitting. During the day I fulfilled a lifetime ambition to go and sit on the infamous Sydney Hill under the old scoreboard, now a listed building, but nevertheless under threat in the never-ending pressure of ground improvements. I had taken my tape recorder to try to record some typically anti-Pom sentiments with perhaps some of the traditional bawdy barracking thrown in but the exercise largely collapsed as I was welcomed into the heart of a genial group who pressed a can of beer into my hand and wanted only to talk about the subject next dearest to their hearts – cricket. They had not, though, been impressed by England's batting that day with the exception of a grittily achieved 99 by Geoff Cook and a rather more boisterous 73 from Ian Gould.

If the Hill has a reputation so, too, does the Sydney taxi driver, and that evening Christopher Martin-Jenkins and I were treated to a discourse on 'that bloody Pom who stays in for five days and doesn't make a run.' Chris Tavaré, it seemed, was becoming a legend.

Monday 22 November

My Saturday night taxi driver should have been at the ground today to see Chris Tavaré confound popular Australian opinion with a splendidly aggressive 147. That innings combined with 77 from Cook and 48 from Randall to transform a first innings deficit of 10 into a target for N.S.W. of 333.

The day had started for me with a report from my breakfast table to the late night Sports Desk (some of the timings were still difficult to work out) on the Australian team for the Second Test. Jeff Thomson was back in place of Alderman, Kepler Wessels was in for Wood and Carl Rackemann was standing by in case Lillee failed to recover from a knee injury.

For the England selectors, too, important decisions had to be made and there was a significant presence in the stand just by our commentary position as Bob Willis and the assistant manager, Norman Gifford, watched a fiery evening burst from Norman Cowans which removed Rick McCosker and caused John Dyson some discomfort.

Tuesday 23 November

Eventually England came out on top – victory by 26 runs allowing a contented party to leave for the airport and the evening flight to Brisbane and none more contented than Eddie Hemmings – omitted from the Test team at Perth and now celebrating five wickets in the day.

An hour's flight up the coast to the north the weather was noticeably warmer and it was pleasant to sit out at a pavement cafe after checking into the hotel and checking in with my office in London as ever.

Thursday 25 November

What a day! It started with a visit to the ABC whose offices had a slightly temporary look about them and, being a series of bungalows, a decidedly tropical air to them. That was in a suburb on one side of Brisbane and Woolloongabba is on the opposite side of the city and that was my next destination to the cricket ground known by most simply as 'The Gabba'. The Secretary at the ground had heard nothing of the BBC's plans to mount a commentary there and was anything but welcoming – an auspicious start! I searched the ground in vain for signs of radio engineers setting up commentary positions. Eventually, the combination of some help from some of the ABC's television people and my memory of a photograph in the first

Test Match Special book helped me to identify our probable perch on a scaffolding platform on top of the three storey building which housed the dressing rooms, the Queensland Cricketers' Club, and the press box. The latter appeared to be a stifling place but that did not seem to be the case with our situation on the roof. I could see straight away that the gusty breeze was going to cause us a few problems.

Back at the hotel at midday the England team was announced, giving me just enough time to report on it to London before going again to the ground for the Australians' afternoon nets. I also picked up the news that Dennis Lillee, out of the Test after an operation on the troublesome knee, would be arriving in Brisbane in the afternoon and had called his own press conference at the Australian team hotel. Back at the Gabba I met at last the ABC engineer who would be controlling our operation and a Telecom engineer installing our telephone – things were beginning to take shape. I had time to interview Kepler Wessels on his first Test cap, Jeff Thomson on his return to the colours and the captain, Greg Chappell, before taking my fifth taxi of the day back to the ABC. In the back of the cab speeding along the expressway beside the Brisbane river I started to scribble my preview reports for the evening satellite circuit to London. As that circuit materialised, I was aware that across the city the Lillee press conference was starting.

That conference was well and truly over when I arrived, breathless, at the hotel, but my luck was in as I could see the object of everyone's attention sitting by the pool with his manager. He was unwilling at first to talk, but a man who has called in the press presumably has something to say and, sure enough, he wanted to make it clear that his career was not at an end. When that interview had been played over to London my shower was very welcoming!

Friday 26 November
In the teeth of an easterly gale Bill Frindall and I tried to settle in on our exposed perch at the Gabba. The first few papers disappeared on the wind before a ball was bowled. We were both going to have our problems. Bill would be keeping his papers to a minimum and I would have to clutch notebook, stopwatch and telephone at the same time to keep Radio 2 up to date. Our commentary was due to start in mid-afternoon (4.30 a.m. in Britain) and so we waited to be joined by the commentators – Fred Trueman, emerging from the Channel 9 box below us, Henry Blofeld and Michael Carey from the sauna that was the press box, and Christopher Martin-Jenkins. . .

THE SECOND TEST
BRISBANE – The start of England's slide.
CHRISTOPHER MARTIN-JENKINS.

I have a great affection for Brisbane. It is true it can be uncomfortably hot, but air-conditioning has banished humidity from the hotels and one can work in casual holiday clothes without feeling one is under-dressed. Queensland is a very relaxed place and if all Australians are warmly welcoming to visiting cricketers or cricket journalists and broadcasters, the banana benders are the most generous and expansive of all.

Brisbane's architecture is, on the whole, an unconsciously vulgar hotch-potch of Colonial and modern. Many of the very modern buildings are inventive and impressive, especially those which cling near to the broad, brown sweep of the Brisbane river which you may cross either by one of the variety of bridges or by a peaceful old ferry which plies every few minutes from the city to Kangaroo Point. As you make this tranquil crossing, sometimes perhaps as the only passenger, the Holdens or the imported cars from Japan (mainly) and Europe (a few) hurtle across the bridges as if tomorrow is coming too fast.

Brisbane is no longer so small a place that everything stops for the Test match, but when the Poms are in town and the Test is on most people know about it and a good many of those cars are on their way to the Gabba. I never make that journey to what is now a magnificently appointed ground, with its smart modern stands, its dazzling orange-blossomed poinciana trees and its grass greyhound track beyond the boundary, and the table full of tropical fruit outside the overcrowded press-box, without a sense of excitement.

The Gabba, otherwise the Woolloongabba or the Brisbane Cricket Ground, was the first major Australian ground I saw and by 1974 it had already become a vastly different place from the stifling, ramshackle ground which earlier generations recall with rather less affection. Sticky was the word for the climate and, when Brisbane hurled down one of her tropical storms and followed it with her customary broiling sunshine, it was the word for the wicket too. In the days of covered pitches, real sticky wickets are phenomena of the past, but the weather caused chaos during the preparations for the 1974 Test and those who were there will forever remember two things about that game: the advent, sudden and violent as one of Brisbane's own storms, of Jeff Thomson, and the amazing sight of the City's Lord Mayor, Clem Jones, strutting purposefully up and down in his wellington boots a few days before the match, 'preparing' a pitch which then looked no more than a strip of mud.

Bob Willis was the only survivor of that 74/75 debacle at the Gabba still to be playing for England (the others still playing regular cricket eight years on were Amiss, Fletcher, Knott, Underwood and Hendrick.) Apart from Willis, Bob Taylor was the only common member of both touring teams but this time at Brisbane there was no doubt that he was first choice wicket-keeper.

England might have been expected to play the same eleven after their promising start to the series at Perth, but it was decided to play a more balanced attack this time – always the best policy – and Hemmings came in for Pringle, who had bowled rather well without much luck in the intervening game against New South Wales in Sydney. The other change was forced by one of those little quirks of fate which can make or mar a career. Geoff Cook had just batted better than anyone at Sydney, scoring runs freely and with great assurance in sharp contrast to a hesitant and unassertive effort in the first Test. Graeme Fowler had failed again at Sydney – nothing had gone right for him in the early weeks of the tour and he had actually been bowled by Trevor Chappell ducking under a slow-medium full-toss – so Cook was preferred again as Tavaré's opening partner. But in the nets the day before the match Cook was hit in the ribs and by the morning of the match was in pain. Enter Fowler for his first Test in Australia.

Thomson's return for Australia was also the result of an injury – the tragic one suffered by Terry Alderman when he tried to rugger tackle an invading spectator in the Perth Test. But there was no Thomson/Lillee partnership because his famous partner was forced to be a spectator after a knee operation. Into Lillee's place came a strapping young man of Viking appearance, Carl Rackemann, leaving Geoff Lawson as the spearhead.

It was Lawson who did the most to win Australia the match in the field. With the bat the man of the match was a 'New Australian'. Keppler Wessels was one of a generation of South African cricketers born, because of politics, to isolation from big international cricket. He played for Orange Free State at 16, joined Sussex and played for them with great success, then made his way to Australia where he was used to strengthen the Australian World Series Cricket team in the two years of Packer Cricket, mainly because Australia were weaker on paper than the Rest of the World. He liked Australia, saw the possibility of working his way into the Test side in due course, settled in Queensland and now, at the age of 25, made such a debut as to make himself a hero overnight.

Wessels had to wait his turn to bat because Chappell put England in again and this time got it right. England lost their openers for 13 and although Lamb, Botham and Randall all got attractive runs in the middle portion of the first day, Lawson's bounce and persistent hostility hounded out six of England's batsmen. 219 was a wholly inadequate total on a good true, fastish pitch.

Our draughty perch above the press box at Brisbane.

Australia's response might have been still more formidable had not Chappell run himself out when in lordly command. As it was Wessels, mixing defence all 'cabined, cribbed and confined' with scintillating cuts, reached a dogged determined hundred in his first Test innings just before stumps were drawn on Saturday night and finished with 162 out of 341. Willis bowled heroically but made some very strange tactical decisions in the field.

In England's second innings we saw some gritty batting against some very fierce bowling. Fowler, enjoying almost as much luck in this one innings as he had misery and ill-fortune earlier in the tour, dug in with a courage which brought back memories of Eddie Paynter, another small Lancastrian left-hander, a hero at Brisbane exactly 50 years before. His most formidable opponent was Rackemann, thundering in with a gale behind him on a distinctly untypical Brisbane afternoon of grey and threatening light. There was much short-pitched bowling, several dropped catches in the slips, and a highly charged excitement round the ground. England went into the rest day only 51 behind with nine second innings wickets left, and those who played golf on the arid course at Indooroopilly talked of a possible second draw.

That prediction grew more confident when England cleared their arrears on a hotter fourth day without losing another wicket. But the Test career of the lion-hearted Thomson was in danger of ending in frustration on the ground where, effectively, it had begun. Many times Thomson has bowled better when challenged by the odds and not only

Trueman, Blofeld and Frindall at Brisbane

was his own future at stake but Australia were now handicapped by the loss of Rackemann, who had limped off with a pulled muscle. Thomson responded with a succession of short, fierce spells, alternating downwind with Lawson whilst the eager off-spinner, Yardley, tied England up at the other end. A mixture of rash strokes, brilliant catches, notably by Marsh (who finished with six in the innings) and determined bowling kept Australia just in the hunt, but no more, throughout an enthralling fourth day. Fowler finished with 83 after nearly six hours at the crease, an experience which either had to mature him overnight, or shatter him for a long time. The signs were that the former was the case. Miller, that infuriating enigma, also played one of those innings when he looks completely at home in Test cricket.

England were 279 for seven going into the final day and with the benefit of hindsight it is not easy to remember how well balanced the game still seemed. Lawson picked up the last three wickets, the last one at least with the aid of one of several painfully obvious umpiring mistakes.

It is no denigration of Bob Willis to say that if Mike Brearley had been in charge of England, listeners to Test Match Special might have had a very much more exciting finish to the match than they did. Mind you, the fates were against Willis. Fowler, losing the ball in the stands, dropped Wessels before he had scored in the first over of the innings – a straightforward knee-high catch to cover, and then Willis, troubled by worn footholds and warned for running through onto the pitch, was forced to bowl round the wicket and could not get into any rhythm. Wessels, reprieved, thrashed him and by lunch after only 13 overs Australia had made 60 of the 188 they needed without losing a wicket.

England came back for the last time into an intriguing match when Norman Cowans was belatedly given a chance to bowl with a newish ball. In partnership with the sturdy Hemmings he bowled fast and well and Australia lost three quick wickets, including Chappell, caught hooking at Cowans whom he had hitherto savaged. But Hookes and Hughes, worthy men and brilliant batsmen both, displayed a maturity born of wide experience and many vicissitudes to steer Australia to victory in the end.

As I say, it was an intriguing Test, but also an eccentric one. The quality of cricket was patchy with many more catches dropped than is usual in modern Tests. Australia missed as many as eight possible chances in England's second innings yet England lost 19 of their 20 wickets in the match to catches. Such statistics almost always speak of too much careless batting. 35 no-balls were recorded in England's second innings, and a good many more scored off. Lawson took eleven wickets, Marsh nine catches. Umpire Bailhache warned Australia for bowling too much short stuff, was not asked to umpire the following match and promptly resigned from the Test panel. Umpire Johnson was embarrassingly proved wrong by a wide margin when judging Chappell to be 'in' when in fact run out in the second innings. Talk of umpires having recourse to video playbacks in future began. In a way all these things made the Brisbane Test something of a microcosm of the series as a whole. It was never for a moment dull and I thoroughly enjoyed it.

The Baxter Diary continued . . .

Thursday 2 December
An early start for the flight 700 miles south to Melbourne, where it was quite a bit cooler as well as presenting a more sedate and decorous image than Brisbane. It was good to see trams and pleasant, leafy public gardens and I liked the old colonial architecture of many of the buildings. Across the park from the team hotel rose massively the great citadel of the world's largest cricket ground – the site of the first ever Test Match – the Melbourne Cricket Ground, better known simply as the M.C.G.

In the afternoon I strolled across to the ground and was impressed and delighted to be warmly welcomed by the Assistant-Secretary of the club, Bryce Thomas, who showed me straight to our Test Match commentary position, where a telephone had already been installed for Saturday's four day game against Victoria.

Saturday 4 December

Cricket at the M.C.G! I was reminded as I took up my draughty position in the top of the pavilion of listening to the commentaries on the 1977 Centenary Test from this ground as I sat with Brian Johnston through the night in a basement studio in Broadcasting House. That box – just behind my present enclosure of two short fixed benches and desks – looked tiny. No room for cakes, letters, etc. in there! The ABC's biggest problem today seemed to be the not inconsiderable one of cramming the substantial frame of the former Victoria and Australia fast bowler, Max Walker into the hutch to take up his duties at their microphone. The expressions of agony on Alan McGilvray's face suggested that a blow or two had struck him in the small of the back.

The pavilion itself – no beautiful structure from the outside – was a fascinating cave of treasures inside. Indeed, I nearly missed the start of play, so engrossed did I become in my guided tour at the hands of the club's librarian. Every corridor is lined with pictures of old teams and in an upper corridor many of the old Victorian state players appear in the ranks of the Australian Rules football teams – that being the game originally devised to keep them fit in the close season.

Stepping outside again into the upper tiers of the huge functional concrete bowl was a return to the 1980's with a vengeance, particularly looking up at the giant television screen which had supplanted the old scoreboard away to our right. It not only performed the duties of its predecessor but provided close up shots of the play and – potentially more controversially – action replays of wickets and good shots. At this stage, with only 5,000 or so in the stadium, reaction to these replays was entirely good natured and it had the great attraction of giving us a second look at some of the strokes played by David Gower in another superlative innings of 88 which was easily the highlight of England's 275.

Sunday 5 December

Who would have thought it could be so cold in an Australian summer? Sitting at the back of the stand I was shivering by the close of a fairly ordinary day's cricket. Graham Yallop made 69 and Julian Wiener 49. The latter fell to a fine catch by Vic Marks at square-leg (one of four victims for Pringle) and the fielder's chance to relive his brilliance on the big screen was removed by his irresistible Somerset colleague, Ian Botham, who placed his huge hands over Marks' eyes.

Tuesday 7 December

Rain in Melbourne was very popular with the drought-stricken locals, but it cast an air of uncertainty over the players on the fourth and last morning of their game. The morning drizzle which had dissuaded me from a pre-breakfast swim eased at about 10 o'clock, but those brought up on cricket in England lingered over our breakfasts and talked of early flights on to Adelaide. At a quarter to 11 I bumped into Bob Willis in a lift in the hotel.

'Any word of an inspection at the ground?' 'They're starting on time,' he replied.

That was a cue for a frantic chase round and a rapid walk through the Yarra Park to arrive just in time to see the first ball bowled, though it was apparent that one or two people – some of them not unconnected with the game in hand – had been taken by surprise by the prompt start. In the end, it was all in vain as the rain returned in the afternoon when Victoria had made 122 of their target of 305. At least Allan Lamb had reached his second century of the tour at the start of the day.

The early finish made our departure for the airport – further from the city centre than most in Australia – a more leisurely affair and after little more than an hour's flight we were looking down on the inviting lights of the South Australian capital – Adelaide. One of the easily distinguishable sights as we came in to land in the twilight was the Adelaide Oval – unusually elongated as we looked down on it. I looked forward to visiting it the next day.

Wednesday 8 December
A 15 minute stroll across the Torrens River and through the riverside park brought me past the back of vine-clad tennis stands to the Adelaide Oval. As I caught my first sight of it with the famous old scoreboard, St. Peter's Cathedral behind it, and the sweep of red-roofed stands opposite it, I was prepared to call it the most attractive Test ground I had ever seen.

From a choice of broadcasting boxes at either end of the ground, I chose the most likely and went to investigate. By chance, the first man I came across there was a Telecom engineer wrestling with a long length of cable. 'I don't suppose you're installing the BBC Radio lines?' I enquired casually. 'You BBC?' he interrogated. I admitted as much. 'Where d'you want it?' he demanded, menacingly. Between us we guessed, in the absence of ABC personnel, which box was ours, but to be safe he left a lot of spare cable for a possible extension.

The box itself was easily the best commentary position of the tour so far except in one regard. From the enclosed hut on a scaffolding structure which supported ABC Television and Radio on either side of us, it was impossible to see the scoreboard without leaning precariously out of the window to crane round to the left. This promised to be a problem.

In the afternoon I took a taxi to the northern suburbs and the large modern ABC building to meet the local sports producer, Noel Bailey, and their travelling cricket producer, Dick Mason, with whom I returned to the ground to have my guessed identification of the box confirmed. The scoreboard problem was to be solved ingeniously by a television camera trained on it, to feed a monitor in the corner of the box. Another problem had arisen. The vital telephone had been thoughtfully installed on the desk in between the two commentary microphones. It would clearly need a very much longer lead.

In India the year before I had been consistently accosted by autograph hunters insisting that I was Mike Brearley. On this tour I had once been approached by another who was sure I was Bob Taylor (he'd obviously seen me behind the stumps). However, on this evening, it was something a little different. As I crossed the road outside the hotel a man came running after me. 'Excuse me,' he panted, 'You are Vladimir Ashkenazy, aren't you?' 'Not as far as I know,' I told him!

Thursday 9 December

The eve of any Test Match is exciting, but somehow the nets beside the immaculate tennis courts behind those elegant stands and their leafy vines provided a perfect stage. A large group had gathered to watch both teams practise, not just press men – although there were several fresh untanned faces amongst them, principally the *Times* correspondent, John Woodcock, who held court and beamed about him at the friendly greetings – but also a large party of English supporters who had arrived under the guidance of Mike Denness to see the last three Tests. It was not just the feeling that England could do with some support that made me glad to see them, but more importantly the fact that Mike was to join our commentary team for this and the remaining Tests.

THE THIRD TEST

ADELAIDE – Another England debacle. *FRED TRUEMAN.*

The Adelaide Oval is possibly the prettiest ground in Australia. It has almost the feel of an English ground with a festival atmosphere during the Test Match. Behind the main stand on one side of the ground tents and gaily coloured sunshades abound on the tennis courts with ladies sporting wide brimmed hats or parasols to protect them from the sun, while their menfolk are in shirtsleeves. This social scene is very much part of the tradition of Adelaide cricket.

On the grassy bank which runs round the other side of the ground things are a bit more noisy. The Australian spectators on the 'hills' love to shout – and they show a ready wit. One new trick they had for us was in their admiration of the girls in the crowd – and there are some beautiful girls there. In the heat they dress very flimsily often in bikinis or very short skirts to the delight of the male section of the crowd. Just in front of the commentary box one group offered marks for the appearance of each beauty who passed in front of them, holding up numbers like judges at a skating rink. The humour can be cruel, as I am sure Messrs Hemmings and Botham – constantly criticised during the tour for their weight – remember. In a later one-day match at Brisbane a pig was released on the playing area with 'Eddie' written on one side and 'Botham' on the other.

On the first morning of the match I had a rather disturbing experience on the way to the ground. My taxi driver looked round at me as I asked to be taken to the ground and enquired, 'Would you be Henry Blofeld?' With no detriment to Henry, I answered, 'Not for all the tea in China!'

After a bit he came back with 'Of course you're not Blofly – you've got too much hair.' Now Henry and I are a little different when it comes to wigs. We carried on talking and by the time we reached the ground he had tumbled to who I was and it was one of the few times I have ever heard an Australian apologise to an Englishman. He said, 'I'm sorry, I realise it's Freddie.' He was really apologetic and went on to talk of the times he had seen me bowl at the Adelaide Oval.

This match was being played earlier than is usual for an Adelaide Test Match. Traditionally it covers Australia Day week-end at the end of January. The bands play and the teams line up on the field in their blazers for the raising of the flag. It was in the midst of these festivities that we played the Test Match here in 1963. We were in the field when the guns in a nearby park started to fire a twenty-one gun salute. After two or three deafening crashes I threw myself to the ground as everyone burst out laughing. After another two rounds I took a white handkerchief out of my pocket and waved it above my head. The crowd really seemed to enjoy it and it made such an impression on them that throughout the rest of that tour I was introduced as the man who waved the white flag at Adelaide.

Adelaide has a lot of other memories for me. In 1958/9 our captain, the present chairman of selectors, Peter May, won the toss and put Australia in to bat. Australia won that match by 10 wickets. So on this occasion when Bob Willis won the toss and asked Australia to bat it was just history repeating itself, although the end result – defeat by eight wickets – was not quite so bad. The intriguing thing was that from the various reports beforehand it seemed that both captains had made up their minds as much as thirty hours before the match started that if they won the toss they would put the opposition in. I found that rather strange, but then there were a number of strange things in that Test Match.

Working for Channel 9 television, as I was, I had a view of the match alternatively from opposite ends of the ground. I would finish my stint in the television box at the city or river end of the long ground and leave the box immediately to go down the ladder and walk to the far end to the ABC boxes which also housed BBC Radio. From the television end I had a view of the magnificent cathedral (after all they say Adelaide is famous for chapels – or Chappells – and cricket) and from the radio box I could see the city across the Torrens river.

After the Brisbane Test we had been joined in the TMS box by Tony Lewis, taking the place of Christopher Martin-Jenkins who had gone home, and Mike Denness making his Test Match debut with us as a summariser, although he had once before been part of the team for a Benson and Hedges Cup Final at Lord's. With the change of time zone our programme times had changed, too. Play was to start at half past midnight British time and so we were taking the first and third sessions. For the first time in the series, then, we were on the air for the first ball of the match.

Bob Willis had won the toss and we all watched in amazement as he put Australia in to bat. By the end of the first day they had made 265 for three, and Greg Chappell had made 115. Kim Hughes looked well set to rub in the agony at 51 not out. The huge crowd had loved it as they basked in the sunshine.

Indeed, by the end of this series all attendance records had been broken – bettering even the 1932/3 tour. I believe English cricket could learn a great deal from the Australian expertise in marketing the game. I was told by the professional marketing men that such is the cricket fever that is raging through Australia that they took in this series more than 1½ million pounds in the souvenirs and bric-a-brac on sale at every ground. Everywhere the Australian public can be seen queuing up to buy, and I am sure that this is as a result of the heavy advertising on television and at the grounds.

On the Saturday of course they came in their thousands to enjoy the slaughter and saw Australia bat on until after tea to make 438. Hughes made 88 and the local state captain, David Hookes, a very popular 37. England made a disastrous start – two wickets down for 21, but at the close were 66 for 2 with Gower and Lamb, who throughout the series had the job with Randall of holding the batting together, still at the crease. The next day throughout a really hot morning we were able to tell listeners in the middle of a British night of the staunch resistance of these two. When we said goodnight to the folks back home at lunchtime they were still together.

I wonder what the reaction of someone waking up ten minutes late for the post-tea session would have been. He would have heard the commentators describing David Gower batting and must have relaxed at first until the awful truth dawned. It was the second innings! In the intervening 130 minutes play, nine wickets had fallen. England had reached 181 for 3 with Gower making 60 and Lamb 82, and then had lost the last seven wickets for 35 runs. England had naturally been asked to follow on, 222 behind. Lawson had taken 4 wickets, Thomson 3 and Hogg 2. Fortunately for those listeners at home there were no more alarms and England reached the close of play and the rest day with Gower and Fowler together at 90 for 1.

The rest day at Adelaide is another great highlight of an Australian tour. For the last 21 years both teams, officials and press have been the guests of Windy Hill-Smith, the owner of Yalumba Wines in the beautiful Barossa Valley about 30 miles north east of the city. It is a slow, winding drive through some beautiful countryside and the hospitality is lavish. On a lawn under the trees a magnificent buffet lunch is served and there is plenty of opportunity to sample the host's excellent wine. For the energetic, there is a swimming pool and a tennis court and many of the guests take the chance of a tour of the cellars. Windy Hill-Smith himself loves to talk of the times he played cricket against such great names as Verity, Larwood, Voce and Jardine. He is a great character.

On this visit, to my delight, I saw across the crowded luncheon lawn the small figure of probably the greatest ever batsman – the immortal Sir Donald Bradman. As always he was surrounded by people anxious to talk to the great man, so I waited a while, but eventually strolled up to him and said, 'How's the living legend?' He replied simply, 'Not bad; how's the other legend?' What an accolade from him! We sat and talked for well over an hour about cricket, our own playing days and watching the game today. Despite being well into his seventies, there is no doubting his crystal clear brain – particularly when the subject is cricket. I saw Bill Frindall and Michael Carey nearby and brought them over to meet the Don. The next morning, back in the commentary box, I found myself on the air with Mike and I reminded him of that meeting. 'When you met Sir Don,' I said, 'I looked at your face and you were like a little boy.' 'I'm not ashamed to admit it,' he replied, 'I felt like a little boy.'

On the field England's misery continued with Fowler going in the second over of the day. There was, however, some splendid resistance from David Gower who made his first hundred for 21 Test Matches and Ian Botham whose 58 was his highest score of the series. Australia's target was only 83 and though Botham dismissed Wessels in his first over it all ended early on the fifth day with a victory for Australia by eight wickets. England were two down with two to play and they would have to raise their game a hundred per cent to take those last two Tests, level the series and keep the Ashes in England, where I believe they rightly belong. It was going to be a real test of character.

Back to the Diary . . .

Wednesday 15 December

Should you ever find yourself in Adelaide when a Test Match has finished early, I can recommend the zoo. Indeed, I very nearly found myself taking up permanent residence there. My wife and I had arrived late in the afternoon and enjoyed the stroll round and particularly the tranquillity of the place. When, at about 6 p.m., we headed for the exit, some of that tranquillity was quickly explained. The zoo had been closed for an hour!

Left Another one-minute report for Radio 2. Peter Baxter at Brisbane.
Right Two living legends – Trueman and Bradman.

Suddenly we realised why the animals had been looking at us as if we were the exhibits. Fortunately we were hailed from a cage near the exit, not by one of the inmates, but by a keeper who was cleaning out the cassowaries. After establishing that we were not anxious to spend the night there he agreed to let us out when he had finished. So we sat there in the evening sunshine under the curious gaze of the rock wallabies until our release.

Thursday 16 December
We left what had become the sweltering heat of Adelaide in the morning for the much cooler island state of Tasmania, changing planes in Melbourne en route. So slick are the connections on Australia's superb internal airline, Ansett, that the pilot had to apologise profusely that the transfer of all the team and press baggage from one plane to the other had delayed the onward flight by an unprecedented five minutes!

It was an alarmingly bumpy landing in Hobart because of the windy conditions which did not make the three-day match due to start on Saturday a very attractive prospect. Indeed, as we battled our way across the tarmac to the terminal building in the teeth of the gale, Robin Jackman said ruefully, 'Guess who'll be bowling the first few overs into the wind!' The landscape around us looked very different from that of continental Australia, or what we had seen of it. Wooded hills surrounded the capital, reminiscent – as was the weather – of Scotland.

Saturday 18 December
Set on a small hill on the edge of the town, the Tasmanian Cricket Association ground is an attractive small arena, mostly for the views it affords of Mount Wellington above to the south and the Derwent River below to the north. To-day, however, the ground's exposed position made it a bleak place. It was very cold and windy, provoking many a comparison with Fenners in April. The bails were blown off three times during the day and hot drinks were taken out to the players in the middle of each session.

These were conditions which made the ABC's commentary position less attractive than it would have been anyway to someone with a bad head for heights. It was set on a tall scaffolding tower at the far end from the pavilion which housed the enclosed press box. Access to the commentators was by a thirty foot near-vertical ladder, up which also was the telephone by which I had to deliver my reports to Radio 2. In between, the press box with its copious supply of hot tea was a much more appealing proposition.

Fortunately when it came to our close of play reports on the Saturday circuit to London, the appalled expression on Henry Blofeld's face when he saw the ladder was enough to melt the engineers' hearts, and they kindly rigged us two microphones in the van below.

Monday 20 December
David Gower had enlivened a potentially pointless game on the previous evening by declaring 132 behind Tasmania. Bowling spells from Cook and Fowler were needed, before Tasmania's captain, Roger Woolley was forced into the position of declaring himself. The target was 264 in 3 hours and 50 minutes and it was achieved in the end with time to spare thanks to the enterprise of Fowler with 66, Miller with 30 and an unbeaten stand of 99 for the fifth wicket between Randall (90 not out) and Gower himself (50 not out).

Wednesday 22 December
A ten o'clock start at the Northern Tasmanian C.A. Ground in Launceston which was a twenty minute taxi ride away from our country house hotel meant an earlier than usual departure. No-one minded because at last it was warm and sunny. Everything about the ground was friendly with one notable exception – the pitch. What should have been a happy day was marred by the felling of Derek Randall, hit in the face by Michael Holding and the doubts raised about the unpredictable nature of the pitch were underlined by the rare sight of Ian Botham in a helmet. He batted splendidly making 56 in England's 4 wicket win which gave me a chance to do all my reports and interviews on the eventful day back at the hotel in mid-afternoon.

I had already been in fairly extensive action. A local radio station had placed its microphones in the press box next to my seat. However their reporter failed to turn up and I found myself relaying regular scores to their studio presenter to the amusement of my colleagues. During the lunch interval an engineer came to check the equipment and enquired of the studio how they were getting on without a reporter. 'Great,' came the answer, 'Some nice old gentleman keeps us up to date with the score!' My colleagues were certainly not going to let me forget that one!

Thursday 23 December
Derek Randall's damaged upper lip was the centre of attention as we gathered at the small Launceston airport for the morning flight to Melbourne. He took the jokes of his team-mates at his more than usually comic appearance in good part and even handled the nagging intrusion of the television cameras on our arrival.

Despite cloud it was noticeably warmer in Melbourne and the parks were full of al fresco office parties under the trees. It was my first realisation of the imminent approach of Christmas and it spurred me down to the city centre for some limited shopping. I was by now adept at the language of Australian shopping in which 'Are you being served, sir?' becomes 'You right, mate?'

Friday 24 December
The absence of Randall from the morning nets at the MCG gave us the hint that he would not be fit to play in the Fourth Test due to start on Boxing Day. That was confirmed later, but at least the practice was enlivened by one joker in the pack. Young Liam Botham joined the ring of players gathered round Bernard Thomas for the limbering up excercises, and if some of the stretches were given rather short shrift, he did at least show himself to be a chip off the old block as he ended up with a bat in his hands flailing at the underarm deliveries from various journalists.

Having delivered my reports on the England team which had Geoff Cook back for the unfortunate Randall, I congratulated myself that I should have at least a 36 hour break before my next piece to London. How wrong can you be! Returning to the hotel late after a dinner out and planning to go out again for the midnight service at the cathedral, I ran into one of the press party who, safe in the knowledge that no papers would appear in England for several days had made an impressive start on the Christmas cheer. 'You've heard that Jesty's on his way out?' he greeted me.

I am not stupid enough to fall for an old trick like that so I took some persuading even to go and check with Doug Insole. However eventually I did, and found to my consternation that it was true. Ringing England from Australia on Christmas Eve is not easy as the annual chat to relations gets under way, but at last I made contact to record a piece for the news. I looked at my watch. It was 1 o'clock on Christmas morning.

Saturday 25 December
Christmas in a large international hotel lacks the personal touches of the home variety and a lot of the bonhomie is slightly forced. Nevertheless the traditional press party for the players held beside the pool was an enjoyable

and well lubricated affair. The players gradually filtered away to prepare themselves for the other tradition of a touring Christmas – their fancy dress lunch. They had to run the gauntlet of several curious spectators as they reappeared. Gould and Pringle first as a punk rocker and a Hell's Angel respectively, Lamb hidden in a pink panther costume and Bernard Thomas more easily recognisable as a Martian complete with radio controlled robot. Robin Jackman looked splendidly authoritative in a colonel's uniform which would have done his father credit, but in military matters he was upstaged by the captain as Napoleon. In the end, Chris Tavaré's unlikely rendering of Hilda Ogden was the winner.

Christmas lunch for most of the rest of us was a juicy steak by the pool and in the evening there was more lavish Australian hospitality – this time at the home of the Melbourne *Age*'s correspondent, Peter McFarline. In the morning we all knew the battle was to be rejoined in earnest.

THE FOURTH TEST
MELBOURNE – The one great triumph. *TONY LEWIS.*

Thursday, 30 December, 1982. Wentworth Hotel, Melbourne, 42nd Floor. Here I am pacing the bedroom, watching the sun come up through its murky overnight blanket. I am nervous. This is ridiculous: just like the old days when I was playing. Will I get runs or won't I? It was ten years ago almost to the day that I watched the sun come up at Delhi, when I was on a 'pair' in my first Test Match.

That is understandable. This is not. Now I am supposed to be the hardened old pro', scribing away for a living and commentating with brutal impartiality for Test Match Special. But England must win today. They must. I open the long window blind with a bit of a clatter and wake my fifteen year old daughter Joanna. 'It's OK,' she says, 'I really want the day to start, because I've got to know the worst. Can England do it d'you think? My tummy is like a tumbledrier.'

'Yes. They should do. I'd always bet against a last wicket pair putting on 74 to win a match. Border is playing well, but Thommo's bound to go soon.'

'You're sure are you?'

'Well it's only what usually happens.'

'No, you're not sure, you see.'

The fifth and final day of the Fourth Test, Australia versus England. Yesterday Australia needed 292 to win the match which would also win the Ashes 3–0. One Test to go. The last pair Allan Border and Jeff Thomson had come together wanting 74 to win. So surely England would win. If we get back to 2–1 and then win at Sydney, we draw the series and retain the Ashes. There is one major snag: Border and Thomson have already put on 37. They need another 37 to win.

Hours later, it is now nine o'clock. We pack our bags ready to fly back to Sydney this afternoon . . . the walk across the park, under the great old trees who have seen it all before, past Captain Cook's cottage. There is a surprising flow of spectators, bustling alongside the Team's Hilton Hotel and across Wellington Parade, and over the Jolimont railway station bridge. I deposit my Union Jack-clutching daughter with friends in the Members'. I climb to the Test Match Special commentary seats, which are simply open benches among the members on the top deck of the Pavilion stand. The full cast assembles – commentators Blofeld, McGilvray, Sheehan, and Lewis: summarisers Trueman and Denness. Producer Peter Baxter is for some reason sitting in the front row with his head in a leather box! Obviously can't face the day ahead, or maybe just watching the ubiquitous Blofeld come and go for the last few months has made him dizzy. Ah well! Many a producer has been driven to the dark room and the cold flannel.

A closer inspection of Baxter reveals that, in fact, he is delivering a minute-long bulletin for London on the prospects of the day's play. The leather box on the head is his studio, his personal protection against the blare of the music which is thundering through the public address system.

Blofeld opens the commentary. He is on the usual tight schedule, but this match should not last long. He performs astonishingly right throughout every day of the series for five radio stations, commentary ball-by-ball for 2UE Sydney, 3UZ Melbourne, 5DN Adelaide; bulletins for 4KQ Brisbane and 6PR Perth. Add to these his twenty minute stints for TMS and it makes about 60 different broadcasts a day. He then adds at close of play his writings for *The Australian, Sportsweek* in Bombay and the *Guardian* in England. Brilliant, breathtaking. He is known in Australia as Blofly. The veritable Superpom. McGilvray makes me worry. He offers to stand down from commentary because it will be fitting for a British commentator, Blofeld or Lewis to be on the air when England win. 'See you've got this sewn up now, you fellas.' McGillers looking puckish is at his most dangerous. *'Timeo Danaos et dona ferentis.'* – I fear the Danaans though their hands proffer gifts. You see I remember the raised warning finger and the alerted eye of my Latin master. But then one ball could be enough; one commentator. Blofly blasts off.

England try to give Border the single at all times to get at Thommo. Melbourne is a big ground and soon Border is pushing for one run but

Left Commentating at Sydney – Trevor, Brian and Bill. *Right* 'Producer Peter Baxter is for some reason sitting with his head in a leather box!'

racing two. Trueman and Lewis censured these tactics yesterday as soon as they began. 'I just don't know what's going off out there' puffs F.S.

15,000 spectators, all let in free, begin to make one helluva noise. Snick, push, paddle, Australia creep closer. Willis and Cowans bowl. Thommo copes with everything. Border who is supposed to be protecting him, sometimes takes a single off the first ball of the over. He does just that off the first ball Bob Willis sends down with the new ball. There's no logic in this game. It reeks of an England defeat.

The odd ball flies over Thommo's middle stump. Lamb might have run out Thommo if Gould, fielding substitute for Fowler, had not run down Lamb trying to run out Thommo, too!

The partnership is 50. Now we think in the commentary seats that an Australian commentator should be on the air to describe their sensational victory. Sheehan takes no pursuading. In his excitement he commentates straight through Henry Blofeld's stint.

Five runs off the new ball and Botham is called on at the southern end, Willis switching. Drinks. Thommo and Border have made 23 off 13 overs. An hour is gone. Australia, 14 to win. A faint chance to Tavaré and a mis-field. Australia need 9 now – single figures!

Through my binoculars I see one sad daughter, chin on hands, surrounded by Australians who are yelling, standing on seats, flag-waving. The Lewis Union Jack is furled under the seat; her camera, hopefully wound on for triumphant action is in the handbag.

Runs are coming quickly, two threes, Paul Sheehan is talking faster and faster and smiling a lot. McGilvray still frowns. Denness eases into 'good loser' intonation on the air. Trueman, soaking wet after Jack Simmons tips a cup of coffee over him still can't understand what's going off out there. Neither can I. Australia are beating the logic of the game. Trueman and Lewis pick up long splinters in large shifting posteriors.

Australia, 4 to win. Botham bowls, Thomson flashes, the snicked ball flies to Tavaré at second slip. Mercy! He drops it. It parries off his hands over his head. But there's Miller. Yes, Miller. Miller has got it! Miller moving from first-slip behind second-slip swoops for the rebound off Tavaré. England have won by 3 runs!

Miller races off the field with the ball. Sheehan stares and then shakes hands all round. A great performance by Border and Thommo. They can't believe they've failed now. They've scored 68 runs on a knife-edge. Death came late and cruelly for them. Look how sad they are. Union Jacks are out all over the ground. British cameras click. Now just wait for Sydney.

Back at the Wentworth Hotel we re-book our flights for the late afternoon, summon a waiter for champagne and drink hefty draughts of Great Western to Willis and Co.

'Cheers.'

'Cheers.'

'You see Pops, I told you it would be a tumbledrier day. Did you tell Henry that I said that? Did he tell you Henry?'

'My dear old thing . . .' Blofeld removed his sunglasses and wiped his eyes and for a rare moment in his professional life was speechless.

Peter Baxter continues his Diary . . .

Friday 31 December

The win at Melbourne had been a great fillip not just for the players, but also for the accompanying press party. Waking up in Sydney the next day one had to pinch oneself to remember the closeness of it all. But the day started with more good news. Brian Johnston had been awarded the OBE in the New Year's honours list. He had arrived in Sydney two days previously to join our commentary team for the final Test, so I was able to ring my congratulations.

Saturday 1 January 1983

If there were any sore heads around after the night's revelry the press showed more signs of them than the players. We watched them in their final net practice before they had to start the next day's task of levelling the series and saving the Ashes. B.J. took me on from there to the famous Bondi beach which inevitably was packed on a Bank Holiday afternoon. But at least I had battled with the Prince of Wales' favourite surf!

A similar battle was involved to find the right ABC studio in the evening with David Gower for a recording for Sport on 2. After sending him back to his hotel I was joined by Tony Lewis for live contributions to Sport on 4 talking from Sydney at seven in the evening to 8 a.m. Britain.

Sunday 2 January

Even at this late stage – the first morning of the match – I had some administrative business to attend to. Some of the commentary team were still without passes. So, early on the morning I negotiated the massive queues – everyone, members, press and officials had to go through the turnstiles – and went to the SCG office. 'I need passes for three of my commentators.' The man behind the desk looked doubtful. 'They're all fairly well known, even here,' I said. 'There's Mike Denness, the old England captain.' Still a glum look. I tried another big gun. 'And Trevor Bailey, the great all-rounder. . .' No sign of yielding in the forbidding countenance. In desperation I tried again. 'How about Brian Johnston?' Across the counter the sun came out. 'Oh, you'll be right, mate!' Three passes were produced without more ado and my powerful cast for the final Test could assemble.

THE FINAL TEST
SYDNEY – A draw – a just result. *TREVOR BAILEY.*

The news of England's sensational victory in the Fourth Test by the somewhat improbable margin of only 3 runs, reached me in Singapore. I was taking, under the Fred Rumsey banner, a party of cricket enthusiasts, by plane to Australia to see the final Test and several limited overs matches.

We were especially delighted by the news, because it greatly increased the significance of the Sydney Test. If England repeated their Melbourne performance, they could retain the Ashes, which, considering they had been consistently outplayed in the early part of the tour, had seemed completely lost. Unfortunately, a second close, and exciting, contest never materialised. It turned out to be an undistinguished game, containing much mundane cricket, some very indifferent umpiring and appropriately ending as a predictable, and rather aimless draw. This was sufficient for Australia to retain the Ashes, which they certainly deserved, and was the extent of Greg Chappell's ambition, as he never appeared to be seriously interested in going for the win which was very much on in the closing stages, especially if one took into account the suspect England tail.

Despite the cricket, I thoroughly enjoyed my stay in Sydney, which turned out to be a hilarious reunion, not only with the Test Match Special team, but also with a host of Australian and English friends. It started at lunchtime on the day of my arrival.

Many people, including my wife, find the 24 hour flight to Australia very exhausting and it takes them some time to become acclimatised and overcome their jet lag. Fortunately, this never happens to me. My remedy is simple. I ignore the lack of sleep and when I arrive in the morning, I simply keep going until at least 10.30 p.m. Exhausted by this time, I sleep through until the next morning when I am more than ready for an Australian breakfast. On this occasion there was a slight problem, because a New Year's Eve party had been arranged. I reckoned that I might have had difficulty keeping awake long enough to see in 1983, so snatched a couple of hours kip after booking into the hotel. Rising at noon, I wandered into the foyer and immediately ran into a formidable trio.

First there was Tim Rice, a keen cricketer with some musical talent, who has demonstrated on Pop Quiz that he would have made a great cricket statistician. Second was Fred Rumsey, who once had a trial for Essex, but did not impress me, a little matter which Fred does bring up occasionally, just about every time we meet. Third was Michael Parkinson, a keen Barnsley football supporter, who worshipped Yorkshire cricket and has also appeared on television! They suggested that I accompanied them to the Royal Sydney Golf Club for lunch and a couple of glasses of Australian champagne, which, like most Australian wine is extremely good. There we were joined by Tony Lewis and family and, after a fairly lengthy lunch, I had a look over the Parkinson pad. It had a magnificent view of the harbour and with neighbours like Kerry Packer, Danny La Rue, and Michael Sangster was rather more spacious, and better appointed than my Southend beach hut!

Returning to the hotel, the Sebel Town House, one of the best in Australia and where the England side were staying, I immediately encountered Henry Blofeld, who had acquired some champagne, French and vintage naturally, which he was proposing to open before dinner. The very least another member of the Test Match Special team could do was to offer to assist, and this made a suitable start to an excellent evening.

I have always believed in celebrating the New Year in the company of friends and this one in Australia proved no exception, because in addition to my lunchtime companions, who should arrive, but Fred Trueman and Veronica, Brian Close and Vivienne, Mike Denness and Molly. The big difference was that at home one normally sings 'Auld Lang Syne' indoors, rather than on the roof of an hotel watching an enormous firework display in Sydney Harbour. However, I confess that I lacked the stamina to join in an assault on the night clubs, which was probably just as well, as the next day my Tasmanian, originally Westcliff, friends flew in to join my wife and myself for two hectic weeks.

The facilities available to Test Match Special in Sydney were different, and rather more primitive than at home. We were not in a box isolated from the general public, but sat in the main stand immediately in front of the Press Box, but it did not matter. What I enjoyed was again being in action with the gang. We had Peter Baxter, our Producer, looking more harassed than usual because his job can become tricky when the lines do not work. Then there was Bill Frindall, the original computer man, who, as he had to share a headphone, was unable to get into the action as frequently as he likes. The rest of the team consisted of commentators, Brian Johnston, Henry Blofeld, Tony Lewis and Alan McGilvray and summarisers, Fred Trueman, Mike Denness and myself. In addition to a son living out there, Brian Johnston had acquired an even larger entourage of associates than usual. This had a considerable advantage, because whenever anybody asked you who so and so was in the large crowd, you could say with a reasonable chance of being correct, 'Oh, he's another friend of Johnners.' The news of the birth of the first Johnston grandson was received from London, while I was broadcasting and passed on immediately. The event was suitably celebrated, and Brian's son, Andrew demonstrated that he has the makings of an excellent wine waiter.

There is a Henry Blofeld fan club in Australia, where he is regarded as a typical Englishman, confirming my suspicions that they really are a strange mob. In addition to his commentaries, Henry was broadcasting on an Australian radio station and appeared to be providing written copy for at least 15 different newspapers throughout the world. The combination meant that he was talking non stop, either on the radio, or phoning copy every moment of the match. He worked so hard that we were worried that he might not be alive this summer to provide us with information on such vital things as buses, butterflies, trains and planes.

The erudition, charm and Welsh lilt which Tony Lewis brings to the Test Match Special team are always an asset, but on this occasion his greatest contribution was being an Honorary Member of the Royal Sydney Golf Club, which meant that we were able to hold our first TMS Dinner in Australia there. It would be hard to find a better setting, or service, wine and food. Although it was a memorable evening, made the more enjoyable by the presence of our wives, it did give me a sleepless night. I brought to Australia the amended copy of the book, *From Larwood to Lillee*, which Fred and I had written. The idea was for Fred to check it. I took this to the dinner with the intention of entrusting it, not, of course to Fred, but to his wife, Veronica. I mentioned the matter to Veronica, put the manuscript down and promptly forgot all about it until I woke in the middle of the night and started to wonder if it – the one and only – had got back to the Trueman abode. I could not phone them to find out as they had just moved to an apartment, a return to the club revealed nothing, and it was not until midday that I ran into Sue Baxter, who

OARD RIGHT			ATTENDANCE: 30,153 NOTES	END - OF		
NG	BALLS	6s/4s		O.	RUNS	V
RÉ (H)						
†9E	1		† Almost played on.	1	3	
			Brian Johnston OBE heard his first	2	7	
S.!W 8	-		grandson had been born an hour ago.	3	8	
R (H) LHB			Grandfather doing well! M1 (NB)NB1			
x9 .!1	4		(NB) NB 2	4	14	
x9 6.4|11	2		(NB) NB 3	5	23	
				5⁵	23	

The new grandfather raises a glass — Brian Johnston at Sydney; and Bill Frindall's record of the event.

confirmed all was well. To me, Sue has never looked more beautiful than at that moment!

Alan McGilvray, that doyen of Australian sports commentators, joined us from his seat in the ABC commentary box, to give his impartial, succinct analysis of the situation out in the middle. He must notice the difference as Australian cricket broadcasts tend to be factually accurate, but somewhat short on humour.

My two fellow summarisers were Fred Trueman, who was distinctly unhappy about some of the bad cricket played by England in the series, and Mike Denness, whom I found especially interesting on batting techniques. Fred was also doing television commentaries on Channel 9 and Mike was looking after a large group of cricket followers from the UK.

Having (before my arrival) been watching and listening to the cricket from Australia, it seemed to me there were two mistakes. First, I could not understand why on television, with only half an hour to cover six hours cricket, they should waste precious time on Tony Greig and a strange machine out on the pitch before start of play. This was fine in Australia, where they televised throughout, but it did not make any sense in England.

Secondly, as far as I am concerned, there is a world of difference between listening to TMS, or any cricket played in this country, and listening to it from abroad. In England it can quicken a two hour journey, provide a background for such things as gardening, ironing, and housework. The scope is occasionally mentioned but is unimportant relatively (except in certain circumstances) and entertainment is a major objective.

Now, I must confess, that though I love cricket, I love my sleep far more, so I am not one of that fanatical breed who stay up all night to listen. I keep my radio by my bed and switch on immediately I wake up. There is then only one thing I want to hear, the score. A brilliant discourse on why inswing bowlers now employ more slips than short-legs may be interesting and illuminating, but, unless somebody remembers to give the score, it will not assuage my demanding need. On one occasion after fifteen nail-biting minutes, I switched over to LBC News and another time my frustration caused me to miss my train.

There is not the same need when the cricket is being played in England, because most listeners have some idea of the situation.

It would be fair to say that, even at home, despite regular prompting from Peter Baxter, we still do not give it quite frequently enough, especially when the commuters are driving back from the office. However, it is an entirely different situation when you go to bed knowing that Tavaré and Gower are at the crease and wake up five hours later to hear that former has taken a single down to third-man and the latter is about to take strike! The news sounds so good that you feel that you can easily manage three shredded wheats; at least until you realise that England have followed on!

The First Day
A disappointing, and desultory first day ended with Australia 138 for 2, which would have been less impressive if Dyson had been adjudged run out in the first over. He failed to reach the crease by such a large margin that it was obvious, even in the stands. For me the most fascinating experience occurred after play had been abandoned and I found myself attempting to return to Sydney from the ground without a car. This is something to be avoided in heavy rain, or after a night match. Fortunately, my problem was solved by a couple of Australian pressmen who gave me a lift to my hotel.

As we stopped at some lights I noticed a bunch of soaking madmen pounding through the streets as the rain bucketed down. Then one of my companions pointed out that the runners were in fact members of the Australian Test team on their way back to the hotel. I tried to imagine myself or any of my contemporaries doing that during a Test and not only failed, but could not stop laughing at the idea.

The Second Day
Australia took their total to 314, including a splendid 89 from Border, who had clearly benefitted from his net in the Melbourne Test. Miller

did appear to be rather fine at first slip to the seamers, as Taylor was covering his left-hand side and Botham, who stood very close at second slip was covering his righthand-side. I remarked to F.S.T. that it was difficult to see how a catch would ever reach him, so that I was not altogether surprised to learn from Bill Frindall that Miller had not taken, or dropped one through the tour, apart from a rebound off Tavaré and he had been permanently stationed there for our quick bowlers!

The Third Day

Despite good innings from Gower and Randall, England only mustered 237, while Thomson took 5 wickets and bowled a remarkable number of no balls which went uncalled. Australia at 90 for 3 were clearly in a strong position.

The Rest Day

Whenever I go to a Test Match at Sydney I invariably meet 'Gammy' Goonesena with whom I played a great deal of first-class cricket in England. The little man from Ceylon was a good, flighty leg-spinner and a useful lower order batsman with a penchant for the cut, who played for Cambridge University, Notts and, after he had settled in Australia, New South Wales. As always Gammy invited my wife and I to lunch and on this occasion promised an Australian style barbecue. This surprised me, because curry is Gammy's culinary speciality. The day turned out to be so hot, over 100, that nobody was allowed to light fires, the barbecue had to be abandoned so we again sampled the Goonesena curry, hot for the very brave, distinctly warm for keen curry men, and mild for the cautious.

The Fourth Day

Australia reached 382, leaving England 460 to win. At 8 for 1 defeat seemed probable and Hemmings, who was to be tomorrow's hero, appeared as Night Watchman, but seemed to have no idea that his job was to stay there and take as much of the bowling as possible. The pitch accepted a certain amount of spin, but confronted by Hughes and Border, probably the two best players of slow bowling in the Australian team, Hemmings and Miller, lacked the necessary penetration.

The Fifth Day

The match ended in a draw with England reaching 314 for 7. This represented a just result, as Australia certainly did not strive hard enough for a victory. Hemmings's performance of the second part of a Night Watchman's job, gathering runs at a reasonable rate, could hardly have been bettered and he was unlucky not to reach a century.

The Baxter Diary concludes . . .

Saturday 8 January

Waking up in the morning I had mixed feelings about the end of the series. There had been times when I had looked forward to this moment, but now that it was here and I had only a couple of days to enjoy Australia before heading back to wintry England, I was hit by the inevitable regrets. Henry Blofeld would be staying on for the helter skelter of the one-day matches and watching cricket while I shivered at home. It had been hard work but what a splendid country to be in. I was determined to make up for the sights I had missed along the way in my last two days. What's more it was my birthday!

AUSTRALIA v ENGLAND 1982–83
STATISTICAL HIGHLIGHTS. *Bill Frindall.*

1st Test – Perth

Norman Cowans became the 500th cricketer to represent England in 586 official Tests and the eighth to gain a first England cap in 1982.

Ian Botham scored his 3,000th run and took his 250th wicket to achieve a unique Test double.

Other personal Test career aggregates achieved in this match were: Bruce Yardley 100 wickets in 28 Tests; John Dyson 1,000 runs in 23 Tests; Geoff Miller 1,000 runs and 50 wickets in 28 Tests. David Gower scored his 10,000th run in the 288th innings of a career begun in 1975.

Chris Tavaré spent 90 minutes with his score on 66 in the first innings and took 63 minutes to score his first run in the second.

England (358) achieved their highest second innings total at Perth. The match produced only the second draw in ten Test matches at the WACA ground.

2nd Test – Brisbane

Queensland, who have still to win a Sheffield Shield title after 50 attempts since entering the competition in 1926–27, contributed five of Australia's team for the first time.

Rodney Marsh became the first to hold 300 catches in Test cricket when he caught Lamb. His six catches in the second innings set a new Ashes record, while his total of nine in the match equalled the Australian record set by Gil Langley at Lord's in 1956.

All England's first innings wickets fell to catches for only the second time in Ashes Tests (Melbourne 1958–59 – 5th Test). They became the first team in Test history to lose 19 wickets in a match to catches.

Kepler Christoffel Wessels (162 and 46), the first South African-born player to represent Australia set a new record aggregate for a first appearance for that country. He became the 13th to score a century in his first Test for Australia.

David Gower (3,000 runs in 46 Tests), Allan Border (1,000 runs in 15 Tests against England), and Derek Randall (1,000 runs in 16 Tests against Australia), all achieved notable aggregates.

Geoff Lawson (11–134) became the first bowler to take eleven wickets in an Ashes Test in Brisbane.

The 52 extras conceded by Australia in the second innings constitute a record for Tests in Australia, while the 35 no-balls not scored off equal the world Test record.

3rd Test – Adelaide

Willis became the third England captain after P. B. H. May (1958–59) and M. H. Denness (1974–75) to elect to field first at Adelaide. All three decisions led to defeat.

Bob Taylor made his 50th dismissal against Australia when he caught Wessels in the first innings and joined the select company of A. F. A. Lilley, T. G. Evans and A. P. E. Knott.

Greg Chappell's hundred was his first in Tests at his birthplace, his 22nd for Australia and his ninth against England. He became the third Australian after C. Hill and D. G. Bradman to score 2,500 runs against England.

Ian Botham scored his 1,000th run in 21 Tests against Australia, and both Ian Botham and David Gower each completed 1,000 runs in Test cricket during 1982.

4th Test – Melbourne

The first Test match to be contested on the relaid portion of the MCG square was the 250th played between Australia (95 wins) and England (83 wins). Three other matches have been abandoned. Melbourne became the first ground to stage 75 Tests.

England's victory equalled the narrowest runs margin established (also in the Fourth Test of an Ashes series), at Manchester in 1902. Playing in his only Test, last man Fred Tate (father of Maurice), joined Wilfred Rhodes with eight runs wanted for victory. To his eternal sorrow he was bowled by Jack Saunders for four.

For the first time in any series, the side winning the toss elected to field in each of the first four Tests. Their dividend: one win, two defeats and one draw.

For the first time in any Test in which all 40 wickets fell, the four innings totals fell within a range of 10 runs. On the same ground in 1974–75, England (242 and 244) drew with Australia (241 and 238–8).

Ian Botham's vital last wicket gave him the fastest double of 100 wickets and 1,000 runs in Tests between England and Australia, in 22 matches. Monty Noble (29 matches) and George Giffen (30) are the only Australians to achieve this feat, while Wilfred Rhodes (37 Tests) is the only other Englishman.

Marsh, who became the first Australian to appear in 90 Tests, took his total of dismissals for the series to 27, and so broke the Test record set in South Africa in 1961–62 by John Waite in five matches against New Zealand. All of Marsh's wickets in this series have fallen to catches and only 12 of his 333 dismissals in Test cricket have been stumped.

During their heroic last-wicket partnership of 70 in 128 minutes, Border and Thomson declined to run 29 comfortable singles.

5th Test – Sydney

Taylor made his 150th Test match dismissal when he caught Dyson, and completed his 1,000 runs and the wicket-keeper's double on the final evening of the series.

Marsh extended his record series aggregate to 28 dismissals – all caught. This was only the fourth drawn Test in 46 matches at Sydney.

AUSTRALIA v ENGLAND 1982-83
STATISTICAL SURVEY OF THE SERIES

AUSTRALIA – BATTING AND FIELDING   (* not out. † plus one 5.)

	TESTS	INNINGS	NOT OUTS	HIGHEST SCORE	RUNS	AVERAGE	100s	50s	6s	4s	MINUTES	BALLS	RUNS/100 BALLS	Ct
K.J. HUGHES	5	8	1	137	469	67.00	1	3	5	42	1445	1159	40	2
D.W. HOOKES	5	8	1	68	344	49.14	–	4	–	46	695	563	61	2
G.S. CHAPPELL	5	10	2	117	389	48.62	2	1	2	49	820	624	62	8
K.C. WESSELS	4	8	0	162	386	48.25	1	1	–	41	1015	729	53	8
A.R. BORDER	5	9	2	89	317	45.28	–	3	1	36	926	736	43	4
J. DYSON	5	10	2	79	283	35.37	–	2	–	26†	1050	707	40	4
B. YARDLEY	5	7	0	53	141	20.14	–	1	–	14	372	302	47	6
R.W. MARSH	5	7	0	53	124	17.71	–	1	–	11	364	300	41	28
G.M. WOOD	1	2	0	29	29	14.50	–	–	–	3	97	78	37	1
G.F. LAWSON	5	8	1	50	98	14.00	–	1	–	8	324	223	44	3
R.M. HOGG	3	5	3	14*	26	13.00	–	–	–	2	123	82	32	–
J.R. THOMSON	4	6	1	21	42	8.40	–	–	–	3	204	137	31	1
C.G. RACKEMANN	1	1	0	4	4	4.00	–	–	–	–	34	30	13	1
D.K. LILLEE	1	1	1	2*	2	–	–	–	–	–	27	19	11	1
T.M. ALDERMAN	1	–	–	–	–	–	–	–	–	–	–	–	–	–
TOTALS	55	90	14	(162)	2654	34.92	4	17	8	281†	7496	5689	47	69

Statistical Survey /2.

ENGLAND - BATTING AND FIELDING

	TESTS	INNINGS	NOT OUTS	HIGHEST SCORE	RUNS	AVERAGE	100s	50s	6s	4s	MINUTES	BALLS	RUNS/ 100 BALLS	CT	
D.W. RANDALL	4	8	0	115	365	45.62	1	2	-	39	860	635	57	3	
D.I. GOWER	5	10	0	114	441	44.10	1	3	-	49	1313	887	50	4	
A.J. LAMB	5	10	0	83	414	41.40	-	4	2	56	1014	743	56	5	
G. FOWLER	3	6	0	83	207	34.50	-	3	-	23	738	515	40	1	
E.E. HEMMINGS	3	6	1	95	157	31.40	-	1	-	9	451	389	40	2	
I.T. BOTHAM	5	10	0	58	270	27.00	-	1	1	39	640	440	61	9	
D.R. PRINGLE	3	6	2	47*	108	27.00	-	-	-	15	445	318	34	-	
C.J. TAVARÉ	5	10	0	89	218	21.80	-	2	-	27	1090	732	30	2	
G. MILLER	5	10	1	60	193	21.44	-	1	-	18	630	467	41	3	
R.W. TAYLOR	5	10	3	37	135	19.28	-	-	-	16	497	325	42	13	
N.G. COWANS	4	7	1	36	68	11.33	-	-	1	9	147	115	59	3	
R.G.D. WILLIS	5	9	3	26	63	10.50	-	-	-	7	254	182	35	4	
G. COOK	3	6	0	26	54	9.00	-	-	-	3	236	170	32	1	
TOTALS	55	108	11	(115)	2693	27.76	2	17	4	310	8315	5918	46	50‡	

(* not out.   ‡ plus one 'ct substitute'.)

No batsman was stumped during the series.

Statistical Survey /3

AUSTRALIA - BOWLING

	OVERS	MAIDENS	RUNS	WICKETS	AVERAGE	BEST ANALYSIS	5 WKTS (INNINGS)	10 WKTS (MATCH)	BALLS/ WICKET	RUNS/ 100 BALLS	NO-BALLS	WIDES
J.R. THOMSON	127.4	22	411	22	18.68	5-50	2	-	35	54	45	3
G.F. LAWSON	230.4	51	687	34	20.20	6-47	4	1	41	50	71	3
R.M. HOGG	107.3	26	302	11	27.45	4-69	-	-	59	47	17	2
B. YARDLEY	292.2	91	793	22	36.04	5-107	1	-	80	45	6	-
D.K. LILLEE	71	25	185	4	46.25	3-96	-	-	107	43	9	2
Also bowled:												
T.M. ALDERMAN	43	15	84	1	84.00	1-84	-	-	258	33	1	-
A.R. BORDER	31	7	71	0	-	-	-	-	-	38	-	-
G.S. CHAPPELL	14.3	3	44	1	44.00	1-8	-	-	87	51	-	2
D.W. HOOKES	8	2	20	0	-	-	-	-	-	42	-	-
C.G. RACKEMANN	33.2	11	96	2	48.00	2-61	-	-	100	48	15	1
TOTALS	959	253	2693	97	27.76	(6-47)	7	1	59	47	164	13

Statistical Survey /4

ENGLAND — BOWLING

	OVERS	MAIDENS	RUNS	WICKETS	AVERAGE	BEST ANALYSIS	5 WKTS (INNINGS)	10 WKTS (MATCH)	BALLS/ WICKET	RUNS/ 100 BALLS	NO-BALLS	WIDES
R.G.D.WILLIS	166.3	28	486	18	27.00	5-66	1	-	56	49	68	-
G. MILLER	171	50	397	13	30.53	4-70	-	-	79	39	-	-
N.G. COWANS	107	14	396	11	36.00	6-77	1	-	58	62	5	1
I.T. BOTHAM	213.5	35	729	18	40.50	4-75	-	-	71	57	-	3
E.E. HEMMINGS	188.3	59	409	9	45.44	3-68	-	-	126	36	1	-
D.R. PRINGLE	73.5	12	214	4	53.50	2-97	-	-	111	48	49	-
Also bowled:												
G. COOK	6	3	23	0	-	-	-	-	-	64	-	-
A.J. LAMB	1	1	0	0	-	-	-	-	-	0	-	-
TOTALS	927.4	202	2654	73	36.35	(6-77)	2	-	76	48	123	4

Comparative scoring rates
ENGLAND   49.78 runs per 100 balls (2946 runs, including 253 extras, off 5918 balls).
AUSTRALIA   49.57 runs per 100 balls (2820 runs, including 166 extras, off 5689 balls).

In the last Ashes series in Australia in 1978/79 the respective rates were 34.33 (England) and 34.30 (Australia).

Comparative bowling rates
ENGLAND   14 overs 3 balls per hour (927.4 overs in 3820 minutes).
AUSTRALIA   13 overs 3 balls per hour (959 overs in 4249 minutes).

WORKING FOR CHANNEL NINE

Fred Trueman

As many viewers who watched the half-hour package of highlights from Australia during the long winter will have realised, apart from the cricketers on the field, there is a very useful team not far away in the commentary box of Channel 9 Television. I was certainly proud to be part of that team, led by the former Australian and New South Wales captain, Richie Benaud, and including Frank Tyson, who now lives in Australia, Keith Stackpole, Bill Lawry, Ian Chappell and Tony Greig.

That high powered team, I believe, gives Channel 9 a head start in the television presentation of cricket, but probably the greatest revolution is the use of no fewer than twelve cameras at a Test Match. Producers and directors in British television would dearly love to have similar resources. With a camera at every imaginable angle no catch or other incident can ever be missed – at least for the replay – and this has produced a new phenomenon. Whenever a wicket falls there is a dash for the bars where the television monitors show the event replayed from every conceivable viewpoint. One aspect about the camera placing which has attracted a lot of discussion is using a pair at each end of the ground, so that every over is viewed from behind the bowler's arm. This gives a better sight of lbw's and catches.

The highly skilled production team of Brian Morelli and David Hill have gone all out to market cricket and popularise it in Australia. I must admit that some of their ideas of the presentation of the game might not always suit the connoisseur. For instance, let us look at that great moment at the start of a Test Match when the two captains walk out together in their blazers to toss. Usually the crowd is in a great state of excitement as the two

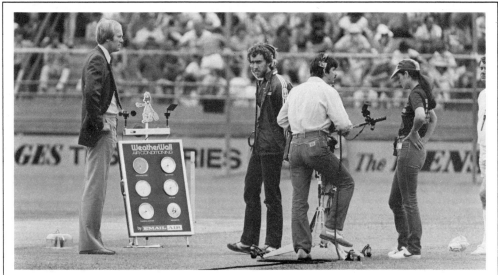

Tony Greig, with his sophisticated team of technicians, awaits the captains for the toss.

men walk – alone – to the middle, holding everyone's attention as they walk the length of the pitch, prod it, and survey it before the coin goes up to a hushed silence.

In Australia that little bit of drama seems to have vanished for ever. Now there are cameras attended by at least half a dozen technical staff out there and before the captains arrive Tony Greig is down on his haunches on the wicket to give his 'weather and pitch' report. He indicates, in close-up, any cracks, the state of the surface, and refers to a strange board covered with dials to reveal the moisture in the pitch, the temperature, wind speed and direction, and the most remarked on – 'player comfort'. Traditionalists hate it all – many converts to cricket in Australia through television think it is marvellous. Greig's performance is followed by the arrival of the two captains – not dramatically alone – but wending their way through the television staff to meet Ian Chappell, who watches them toss in close-up, along with his vast audience, and then interviews them on their decisions. A veil of mystery has been lifted.

One of the earliest controversies about Channel 9 cricket coverage surrounded the use of the microphones which are buried just behind the stumps at each end. I am not sure of the advantage of these, but they do give you the noise of the bowler as he charges in. You can hear the sound of the bat-tapping in the blockhole and, of course, the sound of ball on stumps. To settle the inevitable question – yes, a man sits with a delay switch to eliminate any inadvertent bad language from the players. On two or three occasions during England's last tour he was not quite quick enough – no names, no pack drill!

I have heard, too, plenty of grumbling about the cartoon duck which accompanies any batsman unlucky enough to make nought. Steam comes out of its ears as it turns and walks to the pavilion with the unfortunate player and then it nips in front of him to get through the gate first. Some of the players (and others) certainly feel it is a little childish and do not enjoy the joke.

As now, in Test Matches at home, the commentators have at their fingertips an electronic device which controls an arrow on the screen to point out such things as marks on the pitch or field-placings to viewers. The style of commentary, though, is very different from BBC Television. Channel 9 commentators are encouraged to give something nearer a radio commentary as opposed to television in Britain in which the viewer is left to watch and only receive an occasional comment or explanation. Obviously the presence of advertisements between the overs makes comment at that time impossible. They leave the game for these as soon as the sixth ball is bowled, and return only just in time for the start of the next over. Inside the box the producer sits behind the commentators giving his orders, while the director calls the shots from the van below, speaking to those in the box through their earpieces.

The television boxes in Australia are certainly comfortable. They are air-conditioned, well furnished havens supplied with endless coffee and cold drinks. That was all a contrast during the 82/3 season with our own TMS positions. I would leave this luxury to sit on an often splintered bench with microphones stuck on a shelf in front, and the only copious supply of coffee – at least in Melbourne – came from Jack Simmons, the Lancashire spinner, who succeeded in upsetting the contents of his cup all over me!

Australian television is certainly 'all systems go', but as far as I am concerned they have achieved quite remarkable results. It does not, I know, suit everyone, but Australian cricket was trying to get itself out of the doldrums. Now it is moving very fast (some will probably say too fast) into the commercial world. Without selling itself, the game of cricket will never survive. Unfortunately, as a result, many of the traditions of the game we love may gradually disappear.

CRICKET UNDER THE LIGHTS

Trevor Bailey

Although I once played in a charity exhibition match at Wembley under the lights, my first experience of serious night cricket was in Sydney, during the Kerry Packer revolution. The Australians were playing the Rest of the World in a hard unofficial Test for a large amount of prizemoney and which included a surfeit of bouncers. Play started in the early afternoon and there was a supper interval, followed by an evening session of more than three hours. My reaction was the same as when I had first seen, and played, football under the floodlights. I was instantly impressed, because a new dimension had been brought to the game, which excited me.

Of course, cricket under the lights looked different, as the players were wearing coloured clothing and equipment, which gave a 'show-biz' effect and obviously appealed to television, while the ball was white and the sight screens black. Although I had been brought up on cricket in white clothes and pads, unlike some traditionalists, I had no difficulty in accepting brightly coloured gear at night, where it has obvious practical advantages, quite apart from showing up better on the 'box'. On the other hand, I found the somewhat garish dress provided for the teams in the 1983 triangular limited-overs tournament in Australia both unacceptable and unnecessary when used in day games. The Australian side looked like waiters in a Ruritanian musical comedy, while I kept expecting the English team in their light blue uniforms and floppy white hats to burst into a couple of choruses of 'There is nothing like a dame'.

The other two novelties, the white ball and the black sight screens, were a different matter, because the former had something very definite to offer the spectator and the latter was the natural adjunct. This was immediately

drawn to my attention when I walked onto the Sydney cricket ground for my first taste of World Series cricket. With me was a friend, and life member of Yorkshire C.C.C., who had followed and played cricket all his life. Dennis Lillee was bowling very fast and my companion turned and said:

'That is the first time, Trevor, that I have been able to see the actual flight of the ball from a fast bowler for something like twenty years.'

It was something that had never occurred to me, but unquestionably a white ball is easier for the paying customers to follow, which clearly must benefit a sport wanting to attract big crowds. The white ball also assists television, and television is vital to the game. Cricket in its present form simply could not exist without heavy coverage on the 'box', but conversely, television could certainly exist without cricket. Cricket's dependance is due, not so much to the fees received, though they are important, but because those big commercial sponsorships would otherwise not be forthcoming.

From a viewing angle the white cricket ball is better than the traditional 'red cherry', but it has a serious snag, it tends to lose its colour quickly. To overcome this weakness the Australians in their 50-over one-day matches used one white ball at each end, which encouraged still further the seamers, of whom there are already far too many. Perhaps, the answer lies in a yellow ball. It would certainly be worth carrying out some trials.

Australia, where they do not have our long, light summer evenings, and it is difficult to play cricket after 6 p.m., is ideal for night cricket. It should also be remembered that during the day it can become almost too hot for watching, while in the evening the temperature for both watching and playing is ideal. In addition, most of the working population are unable to see cricket during the day, but can come along to floodlit matches.

A combination of the different clothes, hours of play and commercial marketing have helped to produce a new breed of spectators for the evening matches in Sydney, many of whom know very little about the finer points of cricket. They have come for the excitement, atmosphere and entertainment and have found the limited-overs game particularly well suited to their taste, while in addition, this form automatically produces a definite result, often very close before they depart home.

Limited-overs cricket has taken a long time to catch on in Australia, but now, due to Packer's World Series, it has become extremely popular and is ideal for the floodlights. Vast crowds turned up to watch the triangular Benson & Hedges Cup Series between Australia, England and New Zealand, even though one team had to play the other two an unhealthy five times each in order to reach a three match final, and there was also a great deal of bad cricket. This was perfectly illustrated by England when, having amassed a little matter of 296 for 5, allowed New Zealand to win with several overs to spare, and we are supposed to be the experts!

Australian spectators have always been more boisterous than their rather sedate English counterparts, and barracking has for ever been one of their more popular pastimes. They do not simply barrack the opposition, but

Australia v England at Sydney: the great spectacle of night cricket.

any player who has committed an obvious mistake. The dropped catch was inevitably greeted by: 'Ave a go, yer mug', which tended to become somewhat monotonous. This is why I treasured the occasion when we heard: 'Getta da Bagga, ya mugga', which not only made a pleasant change, but showed the game was beginning to make some impact among new Australians.

Personally, I was inevitably greeted by, 'Ave a go, Bailey, yer mug', before I had even left the pavilion. If I was fortunate enough to remain, depending very much on whose point of view, it became progressively less polite.

Although the occasional drunken brawl has enlivened the Hill at Sydney for more than a hundred years, the behaviour of Australian crowds has deteriorated in the last decade, which is also true at home, especially for one-day matches. In addition to the fights and incessant noise, a barrage of beer cans regularly erupts and an army of tough, and very efficient police have to be in attendance at every big match.

As the evening wears on and the beer slips down, the cacophany increases in volume irrespective of the state of the game, while the number of spectators capable of seeing cricket, even assuming they were interested, is reduced. Although it is neither the setting, nor the cricket, on which I was raised, I find Sydney under the lights enormous fun and certainly intend to go there again.

Night cricket in Australia also makes economic sense and I expect that other major Ovals will follow Sydney's lead and stage evening matches, which could well produce a big increase in professional floodlit cricket. Although the initial installation costs are high, the cricket grounds of Australia, unlike England, are also used for soccer, rugby and Australian rules football, during the winter. These are played right across the cricket square without ruining it. In other words, floodlights could be used for many other purposes in addition to cricket.

In contrast, I cannot see floodlit cricket in England proving more than a novelty, because of climate and cost. The counties did flirt with a tournament on football grounds which, of course, already had lights, but the playing areas were simply not big enough for serious cricket, and it prostituted the game.

THE PRUDENTIAL WORLD CUP – 1983

Peter Baxter

Monday 6 June

The telephone rings. 'Mr. Peter?' a voice enquires. 'I have arrived from Pakistan with five commentators to do ball to ball on the World Cup.' All my elaborate planning is in jeopardy as, conscious of England's own tour to that country in the coming winter, I try to find space, equipment and engineers to cover this last minute request. The anxious Pakistan Broadcasting Corporation producer arrives in my office unwilling to comprehend that here these things take more than just a snap of the fingers to arrange. Gradually we get the first three matches sorted out for him and now he can discuss travel arrangements. 'I have a ticket for all my internal flights,' he announces proudly. 'Please, what is the airport for Lord's?'

Thursday 9 June

At last the day which has been dominating all my thoughts for several months dawns. Getting up at 5.30 a.m. my first anxious look is at the weather. Fine, but cloudy. But then they are not playing any of these matches in Hertfordshire. It is General Election day, but I have taken the precaution with this early start and an inevitable late finish, of arranging a postal vote.

At 9 a.m. after some final work on the tapes which would be our standby in case of rain everywhere, I take the lift down to the Broadcasting House studio two floors underground which will be home for the next two weeks. As the commentary teams head for The Oval, Old Trafford, Trent Bridge and Swansea, the backroom team assembles in its icily air-conditioned bunker just above the Bakerloo line. Tony Earnshaw, the studio manager, will sit beside me trying to interpret my whims as to the choice of commentary venue. Gerry Chalkley, the technical operator, faces a panel of such complexity that his colleagues come to visit it to gape in awe as he feeds commentary to India, Australia, New Zealand, the Caribbean and, at the crackled command of a loudspeaker at his side, to Zimbabwe. Behind me Keith Gordon prepares his tape machines to record the goings on at all four grounds and on the other side of the studio glass Charles Colvile settles in at the microphone arranging *Wisdens,* scorecards and typewriter around him. Tony and Gerry have come through two previous World Cups with me, but for Charles and Keith it is a journey into the unknown.

One by one red lights appear on the switch panel in front of me as the circuits to each ground are connected. There are two commentary positions at each; one for ball-by-ball, the other for reports. Apart from our own Radio 3 programme we shall be serving Radios 2 and 4, the BBC World Service and the various Eastern language services of the BBC.

The preparation time has gone all too soon. I have spoken to the producer and the first commentator at each ground and the clock ticks round to 10.30. '. . . The cricket is introduced by Charles Colvile,' says the Radio 3 announcer. The red light comes on; the button is pressed to play the signature tune and soon Charles is bringing in the grounds for the first news of weather, tosses, and teams. Brian Johnston at the Oval, Tony Cozier at Old Trafford, Henry Blofeld at Trent Bridge and Neil Durden-Smith at Swansea. We are off and running. Instant nerve-racking decisions will still have to be made, but there is no going back now.

Commentary starts with England's opening game – against New Zealand at the Oval where Bill Frindall is installed . . .

ENGLAND v NEW ZEALAND at The Oval, 9 June
Bill Frindall

Election Day dawns noisily in Fortis Green. Jays, magpies, crows, starlings, and pioneer rush-hour traffic compete with the breakfast demands of Bonkers, my manic, white-trimmed, black cat. The great day has arrived – not only for the iron maiden of Finchley but also for the cricketers of England, Australia, West Indies, New Zealand, India, Pakistan, Sri Lanka and Zimbabwe. Today marks the start of the third Prudential World Cup tournament, a crusade which will involve 15 county grounds and be spread over at least 16 days. The 27-match programme will culminate in a grand final at Lord's. West Indies, unbeaten in the two previous tournaments, are favourites to retain the Cup but any of five teams could be playing them on 25 June.

I have chosen to score England's matches in the group stage and they will be playing New Zealand, Pakistan and Sri Lanka twice each to decide which two countries will play the two winners from the other group in the semi-finals. My statistical preparations have been underway since March as my freelance activities involve contributions to the sponsor's information bulletins for the media, to *The Cricketer* and to four national newspapers. Full names, places and dates of birth have been discovered, not without difficulty in several cases, for all 112 players involved, together with such data as what they bowl and if they bat left-handed. The Sri Lankans presented most problems as conflicting spellings, ages and degree of ambidexterity emerged from Colombo. It was a great relief to hear John Vinodhan Bede Jeyarajasingham announce that he wanted to appear as 'V.B. John'.

By 7 a.m. I have bathed, breakfasted, surrendered to the culinary demands of Bonkers, and set off for the polling station. My vote safely cast in the blue corner, I return to prepare my two flasks of black coffee and pack all my books and scoring paraphernalia into two large holdalls. At 8 a.m. I set the milometer on my Audi (it will register over 1500 miles during the next fortnight), and with Sue Bullen (occasional night nursing officer and Essex supporter supreme) as my handmaiden, I join the commuting convoy for a ten-mile trek to Kennington.

Arrival at The Oval has been splendidly cushioned by the kindness of Mickey Croker, Surrey's ground manager. A great friend of TMS, he has provided a pass for the Hobbs Gate, reserved a parking bay and lent me a key to a back door of the pavilion immediately below our box. Thirty years earlier an embryo Bearded Wonder, armed with Tizer bottle, Oxo tin of cheese and beetroot sandwiches, and scorebook, had joined the crocodile queuing to watch Hassett's Australians.

Until it was rebuilt before the 1982 season, the radio commentary box was one of the most cramped and uncomfortable of our potting shed eyries. The new edition has much to commend it – working conditions assume prime importance when one is marooned and working under pressure throughout a nine-hour match.

The team assembles an hour before we go on the air at 10.30 a.m. Brian Johnston, Christopher Martin-Jenkins, Mike Carey, Alan Richards, Trevor Bailey, John Snow and our producer for today, Pat Murphy. Their normal banter is soon diverted by the arrival of John Snow, our 'new boy'. He has adopted the sort of yokel costume that Bernard Miles made famous on stage and screen. Even the beady Johnstonian eye abandons its constant search for cake and jujubes. Snowy is rescued by Sue's arrival with a vast tray of coffee, crockery and biscuits. She is harnessed to a walkie-talkie radio and has been enrolled by the sponsors to assist with the Infotec transmission of full scorecards of all four matches being played today.

Contact is made with Peter Baxter enbunkered in the bowels of Broadcasting House. Charles Colvile, our presenter, makes his opening

Rebuilt for the 1982 season, the new broadcasting box has much to commend it.

announcement and the 1983 Prudential Cup is underway. '960 overs to go', I whisper off mike.

Willis has won the toss and Fowler and Tavaré open against Hadlee and Cairns. After five consecutive defeats in limited-overs matches in Australia and New Zealand during the first three months of the year, England have a few scores to settle against the Kiwis. This is the first time I have operated my scoring system since recording the Sydney Test in January. I pray that there will not be an avalanche of wickets as I regain the sequence of entries rhythm. Although three wickets fall before lunch, including the prize one of David Gower for 39, surprisingly his highest score in Prudential Cup matches, there are no panics. Hadlee, arguably the best opening bowler in all limited-overs cricket, has figures of 7–4–6–0, and England are 119 for 3 after 35 overs.

I always escape from the box at lunchtime for a natural break – such events have to meticulously planned – and a 25-minute meal. Such respites are essential for concentration. Even when I was charting hits and missiles in NATO's war room we had to endure only four-hour shifts.

After lunch all hell is let loose both on the field and in our box. Lamb and Gatting add 93 runs off 12.4 overs in 52 minutes before rain compels the only break in continuity that I am to witness during the whole tournament. During this batting holocaust Pat Murphy, who has had 15 books published in five years, sets a more bizarre record by treading on two different trays of teacups within the same session of play. Mike

Carey, who has retained an extraordinary sense of humour for one compelled to report Derbyshire's matches for two decades, asks if I can recall a parallel feat. I can only offer Brian Johnston's sublime destruction of two cinema seats in the Old Trafford box after a heavy lunch in 1968.

Play restarts and Lamb, with support from Dilley's straight and uncomplicated hitting, reaches a fine hundred and gives England an unassailable total of 322–6. New Zealand lose key wickets in the early stages and are never in the hunt. When one side scores too many or too few in the first innings of an 'instant' match, you inevitably have a dead game on your hands. The death throes are enlivened by a fine innings of 97 by Martin Crowe, whose batting I had admired during my first visit to New Zealand in February. On and on the innings continues without a hope of transforming the inevitable result. I begin to regret the excesses of the previous evening which had found me dressed in full Victorian regalia as master of ceremonies at the Players' Theatre Club music hall for a launch of my 'Guinness Book of Cricket Facts and Feats'. It was 8.07 p.m. by the time New Zealand's last wicket fell to give England revenge by 106 runs. And so to bed.

Peter Baxter writes
England's thunder was rather stolen that first day by the astonishing events at Trent Bridge, where Zimbabwe announced their arrival by beating Australia by 13 runs. In Swansea Pakistan ran up a record score against Sri Lanka, who, while they never seriously looked like achieving their target, nevertheless were only 50 runs short at the end. We had to return to the depths of the studio the next day for what we thought would be a formality of West Indies defeating India. We were wrong. India inflicted on the champions their first ever World Cup defeat by 34 runs. The World Cup had arrived. Two shock results in the first round had ensured the interest in the rest of the tournament.

Saturday 11 June
News of rain around the country was just what I did not want to hear in the morning – particularly not for what looked the day's main attraction, Australia v the West Indies at Headingley. But at least Tony Lewis had taken some sunshine with him on the trip down to cider country . . .

ENGLAND v SRI LANKA at Taunton, 11 June
Tony Lewis

This was the first England international match ever played in Somerset. On the Friday, the day before, the M5 motorway was whizzing with cars carrying Sri Lankan supporters. There were signs in the rear windows 'We come to batter Botham' – pretty aggressive to attack the lion in his own den. The hotels were overflowing. Those who were not too keen on sleep made a prolonged inspection of the Taunton pub kept by Roy Marshall, the former Hampshire and West Indies batsman. My own Saturday began with a rendering of Radio 4's Sport on Four, 'live' from the seats of the low stand, behind the bowler's arm at the Old Pavilion End on the Taunton ground. Scripts were blown about by a chill wind. Fortunately it did not deter my 'studio' guest, a broadcasting lion of the West country, former TMS commentator, Alan Gibson.

The cold got our teeth chattering and froze the lower jaw bone for a while and if Alan, a few days after his sixtieth birthday, took a second or two to 'get off the mark', he was quickly scoring lovely runs all around the wicket. His schoolboy memories were in Taunton and many of the links between Somerset cricket and England were in the ripe old characters, J. C. White, Maurice Tremlett, Arthur Wellard 'who lofted sixes over the stand into the River Tone and who would not move a muscle in the follow through until he had heard the ball splash into the water'. Of Harold Gimblett, an outrageously talented batsman who sadly suffered depressions. A moody man who charmed many lives, but took his own. Alan Gibson had given the address at the funeral service, just over the wall from the ground, in St. James's Church.

Radio contact thus established so early in the morning it was possible to tell the whole country that spectators had begun their queue for this Group A Prudential Cup match at 2.30 a.m. The doors were opened at 9.15.

Sri Lanka had previously lost to Pakistan but in doing so they had broken the record score for a side batting second. England had beaten New Zealand at the Oval. This was a considerable breakthrough because New Zealand had won the previous five one-day encounters during the winter. In New Zealand it was three losses out of three. Sri Lanka, new to Tests, were thought to be easy opponents.

The Sri Lankan coach did sound one warning and plenty of people took notice because that coach was Sir Garfield Sobers. 'They can bat. Their bowling is not good, no depth, but England had better watch out if they do not get a big score.'

England won the toss; they batted and did get a big score, 333 for 9 in the sixty overs. We were treated to a Gower century of breathtaking style and power. Sixes disappeared into the car park over his favourite wide long-on area, missing the expensive looking new pavilion by a red brick or two. Lamb supported with a fifty and the tail lashed violently, Dilley and Gould doing loud damage to a disenchanted Sri Lankan attack.

The opposition did not 'batter Botham' at this stage but they did run out the local lad for a duck. Gatting, who helped in the confusion, then ran himself out.

The best of the Sri Lankan bowlers was De Mel. He is well-built and has a lively action. You could see how the wicket-keeper was sometimes hard pressed to collect the ball cleanly, above waist high. There were several commentary gaffes on the day, not surprisingly when you consider that the Sri Lankan side were newcomers to this country. On radio, Trevor Bailey was said to have called Ranatugna, Rattatunga, and some said later he had modulated even further to Ratatouille! Jim Laker on television did an ellipsis on Dilley and Willis and came up with 'And here comes Dilys, tall and blond . . .' My own contribution was a simple 'Didn't Dilley do well to dig out that Yorkshire!' H'm.

Sri Lanka certainly could bat but they lacked judgement. Taunton is a small ground. It looked a picture; the pitch was good and they could have won the match. They went wrong because they felt that they had to slog once they had played themselves in. There was a fine and most skilful partnership between Wettimuny and Mendis, the former solid and crafty, the latter unleashing a wide repertoire of attacking strokes. Both lost their senses as they saw the overs run out; both saw the gentle off-spin of Vic Marks as salvation and like others who followed, holed out. The one bat-thrower who did come off was the wicket-keeper de Alwis. He was left not out for 58 and there were still two overs available if the innings had been prolonged.

It was in this match that Marks emphasised the merit of slow bowling in one-day cricket. He floated the ball up to the bat, chanced the big hit in order to trap the mis-hitters in the outfield. Willis took a fine catch, Lamb another, Gould got a stumping, Tavaré held another skier and Marks left with figures of 12 overs, 3 maidens, 5 wickets for 39 runs.

The only disappointing performance as far as England were concerned was by Paul Allott. In the opinion of an old England fast bowler who watched him, Peter Loader, Allott was 'not fast enough to do nothing with the ball'. His 12 overs cost 82 runs. It was wonderful to see Taunton so full and so many Sri Lankans on the ground to support their side.

The lasting memory, however, will be of Gower. What a combination of delicacy and power. His late driving, square on the off-side ripped through orthodox field placings. His straight driving down the ground made me wonder if any group of bowlers, mediocre as they were, had ever been so delicately demolished.

Elsewhere play did at last start after lunch with two surprise joint-leaders of Group B hustling through a chilly, damp game at Leicester in which India overcame Zimbabwe by 5 wickets. The matches at Headingley and Edgbaston had to be carried over to Sunday. At least the cricket was worth it as Winston Davis spearheaded the West Indies to a 101-run victory with 7 for 50 and Pakistan never really recovered from being 0 for 3, going down by 52 runs to New Zealand.

Monday 13 June
This was probably the most predictable and one-sided day of the tournament. England disposed of Pakistan by 8 wickets, Australia inflicted a 162 run defeat on India and the West Indies recorded an 8-wicket win over Zimbabwe in the lovely setting of Worcester. Christopher Martin-Jenkins was able to hear about all those as he drove home from Bristol . . .

SRI LANKA v NEW ZEALAND at Bristol, 13 June
Christopher Martin-Jenkins

My visit to Bristol to see Sri Lanka's first World Cup match with New Zealand began inauspiciously.

I had been at Taunton on the Saturday to see England deal authoritatively and attractively with the same Sri Lanka team, and then went to Cardiff on the Sunday to watch Glamorgan winning a low-scoring John Player League match against Yorkshire. Partly because I am fond of the excellent Castle Hotel at Taunton, and partly because two different hotel beds in two nights would probably have led to two stiff necks rather than one, I decided to stay on in Taunton. The result was that I approached the headquarters of Gloucestershire cricket from a different angle from my usual route on Monday morning, and had a rather desperate search around the suburbs before finding my bearings again. All major cricket grounds should be well signposted from all lines of approach. Never mind, I made it in time to see Duleep Mendis win the toss and decide to bat first.

It turned out to be one of the less exciting games of an intriguing World Cup. Sri Lanka, however, got enough runs to keep interest alive for the first three-quarters of the match and there was some good batting by New Zealand at the end to make even the latter stages enjoyable.

The Bristol folk did not support the match in great numbers. I suppose there were about 1,500 people there. But it was a rotten day, if not cold at least distinctly cool, the sky a uniform grey and a stiff breeze blowing all day. Miraculously, and despite confident forecasts that it would rain, we had no more than a drop or two, blown on the wind to make small spots on our commentary box window like spume on a motor-boat windshield.

Our commentary box was one of the more spacious of the ones used in various places for World Cup matches. Its shape was long and narrow, like the old one at Headingley, but the low roof meant that I added several small bruises on my head to counteract the soreness in my stiff neck. Not to be outdone as the prime source of discomfort, the neck fought back when I was doing the commentary because our producer, Anthony Smith, had produced some bar stools for the commentators to sit on. These were fine except for the fact that they were so high, one had to bend one's neck down in order to see through the window!

Tony presided over our efforts all day with an avuncular smile. He is an experienced producer who has been in charge of O.B.'s in the West Country for many years. He looks rather like Terry Scott, the comedian. I enjoyed working with him during the Prudential Cup on what we came to call the West Country circuit: in quick succession we were at Taunton, Bristol and Southampton.

Tony's main responsibility these days is working with Brian Johnston on 'Down Your Way'. For these games, he had an excellent team of Bristol-based O.B. staff and engineers and Caroline showed herself to advantage by getting tea and coffee at suitable times for thirsty commentators. She will clearly go far in the Corporation!

In truth there was nothing much wrong with the box and we were a good deal more comfortable than the press, who were at the match in great numbers in a similar low hut next door to us. I called in on them a couple of times and eavesdropped on earnest conversations about which Sri Lankan was which. Fortunately we had Lucian Wijeysinghe to put us right when ever we were in danger of muddling our Samarasekera's with our Kuruppus.

My other fellow-commentator was Alan Richards, an old friend from the NZBC, a thorough professional with a great sense of humour. In our sessions off mike we caught up with each other's family news – Alan had his wife June over in England with him and one of his sons is living in England, so he was feeling very much at home.

The main memories of the Sri Lankan innings included a brief but good looking innings by Roy Dias (his name a reminder of Portuguese influences on the history of Ceylon) some more good shots by Duleep Mendis, who had played so well at Taunton against England, a brilliant diving outfield catch by Martin Snedden and a sound innings by Ranjan Madugalle. Richard Hadlee, however, was called upon by Geoff Howarth each time the Sri Lankans looked like getting on top and he responded each time with a wicket.

New Zealand's batting on this occasion was impressive. They set out not just to win, but to win by a distance, aware on one hand of the threatening weather and on the other of the fact that they needed to achieve a fast scoring rate in case they should finish level on points with Pakistan, in which case scoring rates would be decisive. In the event they got runs rapidly but not so rapidly as to make up for failures on other occasions, meaning that although they did indeed finish level with Pakistan it was the latter who edged through.

Glenn Turner, full of class strokes – sad to think we in England may have been watching him for the final time in this competition – and John Wright got New Zealand off to a tremendous start and the talented De Mel, who was to undo them a week or so later, bowled much too short at first on Bristol's slow wicket. The leg-spinner De Silva, however, commanded much more respect. New Zealanders do not, it seems, relish unorthodox spin. Howarth played a sparkling innings, not without its moments of luck, but laced with full blooded drives past mid-off and through the covers. He is a good player – on his day very good – and has proved a shrewd captain. The sun began to shine towards the end of his innings but it did not stop the Sri Lankan team looking rather cold and a little forlorn. You would not have thought them very likely to turn the tables a few days later. New Zealand's urgency was appreciated by the local crowd who thoroughly enjoyed the novelty of the occasion. None of the beer-swilling chanting masses were here; just the beer-*supping* county faithful who love their cricket and all that goes with it.

All in all it was a nice, quiet, low-key sort of game. The frenzied excitement could await the later stages of the competition. Halfway along the M4, and homeward bound at a reasonably Godly hour, I realised that my stiff neck had gone too.

Wednesday 15 June

The Prudential Cup had taken sufficient a hold of the public imagination by this time for the Controller of Radio 3 to give us another – previously unscheduled – programme for the two games today. Of most importance was England's second encounter with New Zealand at Edgbaston. At the Oval the West Indies at last found the runs flowing from Viv Richards whose century paved the way for a revenge victory by 66 runs over India. At Edgbaston, England threw away a good start and left Gower on his own to make 92 not out in their 234. Fortunately New Zealand's over rate had been sufficiently good for us to be confident that the game could be finished before Radio 3's cut-off point of seven o'clock. In the end, to our consternation, England's over-rate slowed in the tight finish so that Radio 3 listeners had to miss the final two overs as New Zealand won by two wickets off the penultimate ball.

The following day we had no programme on Radio 3 but found that public interest was still high in Pakistan's 11 run win over Sri Lanka and Australia's 32 run revenge win over Zimbabwe.

Left: Lucian Wijeysinghe, scorer Ian Croxall, Neil Durden-Smith and Colin Milburn with producer Richard Maddock at Derby. *Right*: Peter Baxter and Tony Earnshaw.

Saturday 18 June

Another pair of unusual venues for international cricket made their debuts – Tunbridge Wells and Derby. Lord's and Old Trafford, though, are well used to the sort of excitement they witnessed. In Manchester Graeme Fowler starred on his home ground despite plenty of support for Pakistan, who lost to England by 7 wickets. The scene at a packed Lord's was witnessed by Trevor Bailey . . .

AUSTRALIA v WEST INDIES at Lord's, 18 June
Trevor Bailey

On June 18 Australia met the West Indies, the holders and the firm favourites in the zonal section of the Prudential World Cup. Both had been drawn in what was generally regarded as the easy section, because it also contained India, who had a very undistinguished record in limited-overs cricket in England, while Zimbabwe were largely unknown. The fact that the former had beaten the West Indies in the opening match, and the latter defeated Australia to create the biggest surprise of the competition had not fully registered. I still expected, as I had from the outset, that the West Indies would win their section after playing New Zealand in one semi-final, and that the other would be between England and Australia. The news during the day that India were 17 for 5 and later 78 for 7 against Zimbabwe merely increased the probability, but as New Zealand were struggling against Sri Lanka, it looked as if they would need to beat Pakistan to qualify. Although I rate Kapil Dev as one of the finest three all-rounders in the world, and clearly the best in this particular tournament, because Imran Khan was unable to bowl and Ian Botham's disappointing patch in Australia had continued, the 175 not out which he conjured up to rescue his team from a heavy defeat by Zimbabwe came as something of a surprise. It was certainly the most remarkable, and spectacular, innings of the entire competition.

There is something special about an important match at headquarters of cricket in good weather before a capacity crowd, and the game between Australia and the West Indies was no exception. However, I confess I find going to Lord's for an international game with another country in the England dressing room just a little strange. This proved to be a high scoring and entertaining event, which illustrated the strengths of the two teams.

Even though Winston Davis deputised for Joel Garner, the West Indies had a formidable attack, consisting of four genuine fast bowlers, of whom Marshall was the quickest, plus 12 overs of fairly nebulous off-breaks from Gomes. In these circumstances Australia had reason to be well pleased with a total of 273 from their 60 overs, especially as they lost two wickets early on, and Kim Hughes, probably their only high quality batsman, pulled a muscle running between the wickets, which forced him to use a runner and to miss, with disastrous results, the next game. Hughes contributed a sensible 69, the 56 by Hookes predictably contained some brilliant strokes in between a certain amount of playing and missing. Yallop, who on occasions has looked vulnerable against real pace, batted sensibly for 52 not out and Marsh provided just the right impetus in the closing overs. Although Roberts and Holding have lost some of their speed, they are certainly not easy to slog.

The Lord's pitch was docile and the outfield quick, but 273 still represented a formidable target. The West Indian approach was, however, ideal. They knew the asking rate was approximately four and a half runs per over and their opening pair made sure that they always kept close to it.

In exactly the same situation one can imagine England saying 'What we must have is a sound, solid base, and then with wickets in hand we can accelerate.' These in fact were exactly the tactics which England employed against the West Indies in the last Prudential World Cup Final, when Brearley and Boycott put on 134 runs for the first wicket, but used up 38 overs in the process which put too much pressure on those who followed. Although this strategy sometimes works, the slog does not always come off, while it might be asked why should the later batsmen, and especially the tail, be expected to score at a faster tempo than the opening pair, who presumably are quality players, and are also likely to be confronted by less defensive fields.

Greenidge and Haynes are a good experienced opening pair, who intermingled the occasional boundary with quickly run, and well-judged singles, so that when Haynes departed at 77 there was not only a base, but also an abundance of overs remaining. It was the ideal time for Vivian Richards, the most accomplished strokemaker in the world to arrive, and he proceeded to play another masterful innings. Although the West Indies lost Greenidge for a fine 90 and Gomes who nicked and nudged 15, they cruised home with Richards 95 not out at the helm and overs to spare.

I left Lord's that evening having seen, and enjoyed a good match, even if the West Indian victory had been a little too easy and predictable, but I was also aware that both teams had serious weaknesses, which England ought to capitalise upon when they met Australia in the semi-final, and West Indies in the Final. I still thought the West Indies would probably win, but there were signs that they were certainly beatable. My sympathy went out to Kim Hughes. First, he had been given a limited, and distinctly unbalanced team. Secondly, a number of the players fairly obviously did not approve of his appointment and were not behind him except with a knife. This dislike probably went back to the Packer days. Thirdly, some of the side were past their peak, but imagined they were not only still very good, but also rather special, which probably stemmed from the intense media publicity they received in Australia, which does its utmost to transform limited performers into stars. Fourthly, the side lacked discipline which, apart from anything else, could be seen in the number of wides and no-balls dispensed by their bowlers. Finally, although I have never seen a really good Australian orthodox left-arm match-winning spinner, they still continue to send them to England. I wonder why?

Among the rhododendrons of Tunbridge Wells, meanwhile, remarkable things were happening. India were shattered by Zimbabwe to the point of being 17 for 5. But then came a man called Kapil Dev. And when he had set a new competition record with 175 not out order had been restored and India were able to win if not comfortably at least by 31 runs. At Derby's more prosaic ground New Zealand received a shock on their apparently inevitable progress to the semi-finals. They were beaten by Sri Lanka by 3 wickets. Monday was going to be an important day for some.

Monday 20 June
There was no doubt in our minds as we took our places in the studio where

Mike Denness, Neil Durden-Smith and Christopher Martin-Jenkins at Trent Bridge.

we would have to be for most of our commentary. England and the West Indies were already qualified for the semi-finals but who they would meet was by no means settled.

Our decision was made easier by the one-sided nature of the games at Headingley and Edgbaston. England beat Sri Lanka by 9 wickets and the West Indies went one better; their win over Zimbabwe was by 10 wickets. At Trent Bridge, Zaheer and Imran gave Pakistan enough runs to bowl at, but it was a closerun thing, New Zealand losing their last wicket in the last over to lose by 11 runs. That made Pakistan surprise semi-finalists and we turned our attention to the other remarkable game – at Chelmsford. Henry Blofeld was there . . .

AUSTRALIA v INDIA at Chelmsford, 20 June
Henry Blofeld

One of the many excellent by-products of the 1983 World Cup was that it took international cricket to several of the county grounds for the first time. There were matches at Worcester, Taunton, Chelmsford, Derby, Bristol, Leicester and Southampton, and they all aroused tremendous local interest.

I was lucky enough to go to Chelmsford where the ground had been sold out for some days, to watch Australia play India in a game which decided which of the two would go through to the semi-finals.

The occasion, watched by 8,000 people, was as memorable as the match itself which produced a convincing victory for India by 118 runs, in a week which saw them outplay Australia, England and then the West Indies in the final at Lord's.

Peter Edwards, the secretary of Essex, had coped splendidly with the many problems involved in turning a county ground into an international venue for one day. When I ran into him during the day, he said with a smile, 'It's never like this when Essex are playing Glamorgan on a Monday'.

Chelmsford is a charming county ground which personifies county cricket in Essex just as Taunton does with Somerset cricket. At one end there is a causeway where the dual carriageway funnels traffic into and out of the town; the river Chelmer flows down one side behind the pavilion, the local hospital sits on the other side of the ground behind the scoreboard, and behind the hedge at the far end there are the colourful gardens of the neighbouring houses.

I caught the nine o'clock train down from Liverpool Street and at the end of the five minute walk from the station, I found the ground almost full although there was an hour to go before the start. Already, there was a strong Indian contingent which helped give the day a more vibrant and exciting atmosphere.

Appropriately, an announcement came over the public address system soon after the start, that the special dish the caterers were providing for lunch was curry, which brought loud cheers! In the closing stages of the match the noise which included the blowing of trumpets and bugles but not, mercifully, the letting off of fire crackers, from the stand on the right of the commentary box, made me think that I was watching a game at Eden Gardens, Calcutta.

At Chelmsford the new BBC commentary box is situated on the second tier of the new stand behind the bowler's arm at the Causeway end. It is admirable for county matches when there is never more than one commentator and a scorer.

Now, we had three commentators, Brian Johnston, Jim Maxwell from the ABC, and myself, two summarisers, Trevor Bailey and Farokh Engineer – I can't think what we would have done had one been Colin Milburn – our scorer, Peter Byrne and our producer, Joanne Watson. Getting into and out of the box at the beginning and end of every commentary spell made an SAS assault course look like question one.

BJ was in his best form and started off the day with two quick fire funnies to Farokh. A woman went into the local town hall and asked the commissionaire the way to the office for pubic affairs. 'I think you mean public affairs madame,' the commissionaire replied. 'Oh no I don't,' she came back, 'this is a strictly private matter.'

Farokh was unable to answer the question about who was the fastest man on two wheels in London. BJ supplied the answer, 'an Arab riding a bicycle through Golders Green.'

Then came the more serious stuff. Kim Hughes's leg had not mended and so David Hookes captained Australia for the first time, while all-rounder Ken Macleay came into the side. Another Australian change was the replacement of Dennis Lillee by Geoff Lawson which meant that Lillee had probably played his last game for Australia in England. Kirti Azad took Ravi Shastri's place in the Indian side.

Kapil Dev then won the toss for India and decided to bat on what looked a pretty good pitch. Although Australia did not bowl especially well and Rodney Hogg sent down a total of fifteen no-balls which is unforgivable in limited over cricket particularly from such an experienced bowler, wickets fell steadily.

All the main Indian batsmen did the hard work and played themselves in, but they all then got themselves out and a total of 247 was neither quite one thing nor the other. On a good pitch I did not think it would give Australia all that much of a problem.

But this was not a happy Australian side; things had been going against them from the moment they lost their first match to Zimbabwe and there were obviously several factions pulling in opposite directions in their dressing room.

They made a bad start now when Trevor Chappell was caught in the gully in Madan Lal's first over, but Graeme Wood and Graham Yallop then began to bat well and they had 40 on the board in the fourteenth over and Australia looked to have things under control.

But suddenly their batting disintegrated in the most extraordinary way. In Roger Binny's first over, Wood played forward and was bowled, Hookes played a ball into his stumps in Binny's second over and in his third, Yallop tried to hook and skied a catch back to the bowler. The noise from the Indian contingent in the crowd was deafening and one gentleman with a trumpet must have come close to bursting his lungs.

Yallop had been out to the last ball of the over and, the batsmen having crossed, Rod Marsh now faced Madan Lal. He played half-forward to his first ball and was lbw. Macleay was sixth out at 69 driving at Madan Lal and being caught at slip, and that was effectively that. Australia were all out for 129. India won by 118 runs and went up to Old Trafford to beat England in the semi-final.

It was a good day in the commentary box even if the sponsors temporarily lost our lunches and when they arrived we were short on implements, but our BBC training enabled us to improvise.

I did not know what lay in store for me at Old Trafford two days later when during a commentary spell Farokh suddenly asked me how I got on with the lovely maidens in Bombay. I think I won the point when I replied that I had once seen Nadkarni bowl twelve maiden overs in succession. The fact that it had been at Madras and not Bombay was irrelevant!

In the Old Trafford semi-final I got into a bad double entendre too. Towards the end when England were clearly beaten, I was describing the row of press photographers on the grass in front of the commentary box. I told listeners that the one on the left was Patrick Eagar who had produced so many marvellous books of cricket photographs. I went on to say that he had his eye to the lens, his finger on the button and he was sitting on his equipment which reduced the inhabitants of our box to jelly in a matter of moments. It was difficult to continue commentary!

Back at Chelmsford, I had one personal problem for we had no Direct Exchange Line, a normal telephone, in the control caravan, and in order to do my telephoned broadcasts back to Australia I had to go round to the sponsors office in the indoor cricket school. Once again the man from the Pru had come to my aid, but in this case it was a lovely lady from the Pru.

During the day we had a visit in the box from one of our warmest supporters, Morag Brownlow who was in effect a special emissary from the former Maharajah of Baroda, another great friend of, and contributor to, TMS. The Prince was going to call Morag and Claude Brownlow that evening from Bombay for a blow by blow account which I know will have delighted him.

My final memory of a glorious day was standing on the players balcony with the Indian High Commissioner to Great Britain and Raj Singh, a former Indian selector, who had managed the tour to England in 1982, while waiting to interview Kapil Dev. Understandably, they were both extremely buoyant and the Indian players, too.

In sharp contrast, the Australians, carrying their cricket bags, slipped away unnoticed to the team coach for the journey back to London and eventually Australia. A good many Indian spectators stayed down on the ground in front of the pavilion shouting for their heroes as the light grew dim and Chelmsford then returned once again to a county ground after a heady day in the sun.

ENGLAND v INDIA – SEMI-FINAL at Old Trafford, 22 June
Trevor Bailey

The experimental opening pair of Tavaré and Fowler provided England with an unexpectedly boisterous start against India in the semi-final at Old Trafford, in fact the speed of their running between the wickets combined with the rate that runs were being accumulated resembled a genuine gallop which promised a massive score. Although both were victims of Binny the prospects of a large total remained good, until Kapil Dev, fearing this, decided to introduce his fifth and sixth bowlers,

Azad and Amarnath, in double-harness for the quiet period before lunch, in order to use up some of their overs before the afternoon acceleration. This proved an inspired move, because the latter had Gower caught off a lazy shot and after lunch they becalmed a sub-standard England middle order, so that from the prosperity of 107 for 2 they were all out for a disappointing 213. Then, India for the only time in their great week demonstrated, or indeed, as events turned out, relied on their batting prowess. Against England they batted their way to a most convincing victory with plenty of wickets and runs in hand.

Why were the Indian bowlers so successful? Apart from Kapil Dev who is a world-class player, it is difficult to think of the other four as much more than adequate. It is unlikely that Madan Lal, Sandhu, Binny, or Amarnath would have claimed a place in the England team for their bowling and we certainly do not possess an outstanding attack. The first three looked no more than the third seamers in a county side and Amarnath a fourth.

One reason, and perhaps the most important, why their seamers did so well, was that they were all better than the opposition realised. They had been brought up on good batting pitches where they had to learn how to do a little with the ball and maintain a line and length, or otherwise they would have become cannon fodder for the batsmen who all have insatiable appetites for runs. As a result in England, where conditions are more helpful to seam bowling, they thrived. All credit to them, for being responsible for India bringing off one of cricket's greatest surprises.

WEST INDIES v PAKISTAN – SEMI-FINAL at the Oval, 22 June
Fred Trueman

Forcing my way through the crowds outside the gates of the Oval an hour before the start of play I felt I might have been in Port of Spain or Karachi. As an Englishman, I began to feel I was in the wrong place. The talk was all foreign to me with a desperate clamouring for tickets. Prices between £25 and £50 were being offered. As I was recognised people called out to me for tickets, but I could not help them as I reached the Hobbs Gates leaving the chaos outside.

A strong team was assembled in the splendid new commentary box at the top of the pavilion – Christopher Martin-Jenkins and the inevitable Brian Johnston, Tony Cozier representing the West Indies, and Mushtaq Mohammad representing Pakistan. With Radio 3 obviously more interested in the England semi-final at Old Trafford we started commentary a few minutes before the game started for the thousands listening eagerly in the Caribbean. The view from those new boxes is excellent and greatly impressed my newspaper sports editor who I showed round. I sometimes think we have a better view than the umpire as we are not only straight behind the wicket, but we are also in an elevated position. For commentary, it is perfect.

Johnners kicked off, describing the West Indies having won the toss and as usual in cloudy but warm and sticky conditions putting Pakistan in to bat. The forecast said it would clear and we would have a sunny afternoon (it turned out to be right) so it was the ideal situation for the West Indian pace battery of Roberts, Holding, Marshall and Garner to get to work. Garner particularly found uneven bounce in the dry brown pitch and throughout the morning session batting was very difficult with plenty of playing and missing. After a slow start they found themselves 34 for two when Zaheer joined Mohsin Khan. They pulled Pakistan back into the game but shortly before lunch Zaheer got himself out, bowled playing a rash stroke as he danced out to attack Gomes.

The West Indies were taking control despite a fine responsible innings from Mohsin, who got out not long before the end for 70. Pakistan had made 183 for 8.

The West Indies started their innings in the forecast sunshine. The ball had stopped swinging, the dampness was out of the pitch and conditions were ideal. With the Pakistan fast attack no more than a pop-gun beside the West Indian artillery, the batsmen found it a comfortable task to reach their target of 185. Along the way they lost Greenidge and Haynes but that just brought in Richards who had made a hundred here against India a week before. This was a majestic display played more like a Test Match than a one-day innings. He took his time and just coasted his way to 80 not out with an effortless undefeated half century from Gomes at the other end.

It had become a very one-sided affair and not a match worthy of a semi-final in such a wonderful competition as this had turned out to be. Any Pakistan supporter would have to be disappointed in the showing of their batting line up which looked so powerful on paper. Johnners was teasing me gently about my decision of the man of the match as I was the day's adjudicator. I would not tell him of course, but I was thinking of giving it to Mohsin Khan, because although he made ten runs fewer than Viv Richards he did it against a better attack in more difficult conditions. In the end, though, the Pakistan team did not bother to turn up on the balcony after the game, so I gave it to Richards, which seemed a popular choice.

One thing really disturbed me as an Englishman. News of the fall of England wickets at Old Trafford was cheered in the crowd who stayed on to watch their defeat by India on the giant screen from Twickenham installed here for the season. Again I felt like a foreigner in my own land.

THE FINAL AT LORD'S – Saturday 27 June
Brian Johnston

What a tournament! What a jamboree! What fun! What weather! What a success! What a grand climax! I still cannot believe it. I shall never forget the scenes at the end when at 7.25 p.m., Holding was lbw to Amarnath, and India had beaten the West Indies by 43 runs. The hordes of Indian supporters leapt out of their starting blocks, and swept across the ground in a stampede, as they rushed towards the pavilion with flags and banners waving proudly on high. Players and umpires got caught up in the tide of humanity, and poor Holding was knocked over and trampled on in the crush. The tournament itself was by far the most successful of the three held so far. Each side having to play the other twice made a big difference. Except for a couple of hiccups in the early days, the weather was near perfect for a fortnight – and that after thirty-six consecutive days of rain in May and early June. Eight teams made up of one hundred and twelve players were brought together. Favourites were toppled. Underdogs turned dramatic tables. No side was undefeated. In fact the feature of the tournament was the evenness of the teams.

The fifteen grounds used were packed with enthusiastic and unashamedly partisan spectators. Two hundred and fifty thousand of them watched the matches, and paid £1,200,000 to do so. When added to the generous sponsorship of the Prudential this meant that there was a million pounds to distribute to the eight cricketing countries. It was a massive operation for radio. On the eve of the tournament all the commentators and summarisers assembled for a reception at the Cricketers Club. Many met for the first time and it was fun to meet the body containing what, up to that moment, had just been a voice from some far-off cricket ground. Altogether twenty commentators and eleven summarisers took part, and every one of the twenty-seven matches was covered, either by ball-by-ball commentary or by live reports as things happened. Throughout, there were broadcasts to Australia, the Caribbean, New Zealand, India, Pakistan, Sri Lanka, and Zimbabwe, and to the rest of the world via the special BBC World Service cricket transmission. On the final day we were joined by South Africa, and Bermuda, and it was estimated to be our biggest cricket radio audience ever – probably with one hundred million listeners.

India's performance was remarkable. Starting at odds of 33–1, no-one gave them a chance. Too many of us had memories of their first-ever Prudential match at Lord's in 1975 when Gavaskar batted throughout India's sixty overs for only 36 not out. But people soon sat up and took notice when in their first match in this tournament India beat the West Indies at Old Trafford. They were also to go on and beat Australia and

Back row, left to right: Ian Davies, Neil Durden-Smith, John Snow, Christopher Martin-Jenkins, Peter Walker, Peter Richardson, Peter Parfitt, Fred Titmus, Brian Johnston. *Middle row sitting, left to right:* Fred Trueman, Colin Milburn, Bob Nixon, Rachael Heyhoe-Flint, Don Mosey, Alan Richards, Lucian Wijeysinghe, Jim Maxwell, Norman Cuddeford. *Front row, left to right:* Ralph Dellor, Michael Carey, Tony Cozier, Farokh Engineer, Trevor Bailey, Mushtaq Mohammad, Mike Denness.

England to prove what a very different side they are today. Their batsmen have learnt to attack fast bowlers, their fielding is vastly improved and their innocent looking bowlers are an example to all the other competing countries. All of them except Kapil Dev are medium-pace but they bowl a line and length, and in this country particularly get their reward, because the ball will usually help them in the air or off the pitch. But perhaps the most noticeable change was in their captaincy. Twenty-four-year-old Kapil Dev has welded them into a team. On the field he encourages, cajoles, and sympathises. He leads from the front. His fielding is an example to all his players. His 303 runs and 12 wickets in the tournament speak for themselves. He has done for India what Frank Worrell did for the West Indies – and he was personally responsible for the vital innings of the whole tournament. It kept India with a chance of reaching the semi-final when all seemed lost against Zimbabwe at Tunbridge Wells.

My fear was that not enough Indians would be at Lord's for the final. After all, the match had been a sell-out for two months before, and it seemed to me unlikely that many Indians would then have had sufficient confidence in their team to invest in a ticket so far in advance. In St. John's Wood we have many friendly Indians who run the post offices, food stores and greengrocers. After their win at Old Trafford I was asked for tickets wherever I went in the 'Wood'. In fact, at 7 a.m. on the morning of the final a boy from the paper-shop knocked on our door and pleaded for a ticket.

As I walked to the ground past Paul McCartney's house in Cavendish Avenue, I saw my worst fears realised. There was a long tail of cars stretching round the streets. People with tickets were wrapped round the ground waiting to go through the turnstiles. Even the members had a queue a quarter of a mile long round the corner from the Grace Gates down Grove End Road. But far worse were the thousands of Indians milling around and massed outside the gates at the Nursery end. I have not seen bigger crowds at Lord's since the 1953 Test against Australia when 10,000 were shut out of the ground.

Somehow, thank goodness, many of the Indian supporters did manage to get in. I fear many had to pay the ticket touts, and my fruit-monger told me that tickets were selling for £30 or £40. But, be that as it may, by the time the match started there were thousands of Indians inside the ground – many of them sitting on the grass under the Grandstand.

As usual, I got there early, at 9 o'clock, just before the gates opened. I had two appointments before going up to the commentary box. I had promised to meet and chat to an enthusiastic eleven-year-old named Timothy Mills outside the door of the pavilion. Then I had a quick meeting with the Riff Raff Club – a band of keen cricket watchers of whom I am proud to be President. Only two of the twelve had managed to get through the crowd in time. But they were the vital ones because they brought with them a delicious white iced cake made by Alison, one of the wives. This was a present for my birthday which had been the day before. It was a great start to the day and was supplemented by three ice-cold bottles of Bollinger kindly brought round to the pavilion by a friend named Anthony Lieschallas. So I was pretty popular as I arrived in the commentary box. As usual, the Bearded Wonder was the first arrival, after Peter Baxter and the four engineers who were to send out our words to the world.

There was a sense of the big occasion in the box and we had a full complement of TMS team of commentators and summarisers, including Farokh Engineer, to represent India. Throughout the day the box was full to overflowing. At one time I counted twenty people including welcome visitors like Hanif Mohammad and Bert Sutcliffe – not a bad opening pair! We made no secret of our belief that West Indies would win. We all just prayed that India would put up a fight and make a match of it. Our hearts sank when we saw that Clive Lloyd had won the toss and put India in. It was worse when, in the first over we saw that exciting stroke-player, Shrikkanth offer the left cheek of his bottom to two short-pitched balls outside the leg-stump from Andy Roberts; normally, he would have hooked them into the Grandstand. Had someone 'got' at him and told him to cut out his strokes on this great occasion?

We need not have worried. He was soon his brilliant self, hitting a six and seven fours in his 38 which, remarkably, was to be the top score of the match. His fellow batsmen followed his example and with five sixes into the Grandstand perhaps played too freely. A total of 183 looked a push-over for West Indies although everyone admired the spirit of the Indian batsmen.

During the luncheon interval I had gone down to join my family at the picnic area behind the Warner Stand. I have never seen it more crowded – every blade of grass was occupied with picnickers eating their strawberries to the accompaniment of popping corks. Already with the lunch score, India 92 for 4, heads were shaking as people bemoaned the fact that it was going to be a non-match. At least, they said, let us hope that India make enough so that we can see a big innings from Viv Richards. On my way back to the pavilion a lady stopped me and asked for my autograph. 'Clever of you to recognise me', I said. 'Oh', she replied, 'I recognised your voice before you even spoke!' It was after the West Indies had been patting about for almost fifty minutes that it suddenly began to dawn on the crowd that they might be watching a tale of the unexpected. Greenidge had gone for 1, offering no stroke; Haynes had been caught in the covers, and Richards, who had come to Lord's with an average of 83.00, had charmed the crowd with his masterly timing and stoke-play, and had made 33 with seven fours.

At 57 for 2 the only worry for West Indies was that Clive Lloyd had pulled his injured groin muscle playing his first stroke. He had Haynes as a runner, but was severely restricted in his foot movements. It was at this point that a possibly too confident Richards tried to hit Madan Lal into the Grandstand over mid-wicket. He skied the ball, and Kapil Dev running towards the Grandstand made a super catch. Richards gone, a limping Lloyd, and at 57 for 3, the atmosphere round the ground began to change. The drums of the West Indian supporters from the Tavern and Mound Stand areas became muffled. The horns and whistles for India took over with a continuous cacophany of ear-piercing noise. In the commentary box the experts began to hedge. Those writing for newspapers began to re-write, and at the tea score of 76 for 5 off 25 overs, Farokh Engineer rushed down to the Indian dressing-room to congratulate his fellow countrymen and urge them to keep calm. But as wickets began to fall, Farokh failed to follow his own advice! He got more and more excited. His eyes were flashing and his voice raised in excitement. Even a stubborn stand of 43 for the 7th wicket between Dujon and Marshall, failed to sap his confidence. In contrast, Tony Cozier was showing much less of his usual exuberance. We made sure that Farokh was at the microphone as the inevitable Indian victory approached. He jumped up and down in his seat. A microphone was hardly necessary. I'm sure they could have heard his voice in India without it. When Holding was lbw to Amarnath and West Indies were all out for 140, it was absolute bedlam in the box. Farokh called on Mrs Gandhi – he was sure she was listening – to announce a public holiday immediately. This was a great moment for India and indeed for cricket; the scenes in front of the pavilion were fantastic. This was the final proof that thousands of Indians had, after all, been able to get tickets. Indian banners were everywhere, one announcing that Kapil Dev was the Curry King. But what was so nice was the sporting way all the West Indian supporters took their defeat, especially Tony Cozier, who must have been desperately disappointed. It had been a long day in the box. But what a day, and what a turn-up! Behind his pipe Fred was busy re-writing his piece for *The People* for the third time and muttering under his breath that 'cricket is a funny game'.

For once, I did not make the pun of the match. That doubtful honour fell to Trevor Bailey. I was describing an Indian fielder in a white floppy hat chasing a ball down at the Nursery End. 'I'm not quite sure who it is under that hat', I said, 'I think its Azad'. 'Yes', said The Boil, 'I'll Azad a guess that you are right.' '. . . No comment!'

INDIA INNINGS v WEST INDIES — 1983 PRUDENTIAL CUP FINAL at LORD'S on 25 JUNE. TOSS: WEST INDIES

IN	OUT	MINS	No.	BATSMAN	HOW OUT	BOWLER	RUNS	WKT	TOTAL	6s	4s	BALLS	NOTES ON DISMISSAL	OVER OUT
10.45	10.58	13	1	S.M.GAVASKAR	C† DUJON	ROBERTS	2	1	2	·	·	12	Followed ball that left him - firm-footed stroke.	5
10.45	12.06	81	2	K.SRIKKANTH	LBW	MARSHALL	38	2	59	1	7	57	Hit across line - beaten by pace.	19
11.00	12.48	108	3	M.AMARNATH	BOWLED	HOLDING	26	3	90	·	3	80	Missed offside steer at ball which hit off stump.	30
12.08	12.53	45	4	YASHPAL SHARMA	C† SUB (A.L.LOGIE)	GOMES	11	4	92	·	1	32	Scooped easy catch to deep cover.	31
12.50	2.17	45	5	S.M.PATIL	C† GOMES	GARNER	27	8	153	1	·	29	Mistimed hook - misjudged bounce - simple mid-on catch.	42
12.55	1.44	8	6	KAPIL DEV*	C† HOLDING	GOMES	15	5	110	·	3	8	Drove skier to long-on.	33
1.46	1.47	1	7	K.AZAD	C† GARNER	ROBERTS	0	6	111	·	·	3	Hooked long-hop to backward square-leg.	34
1.49	1.58	9	8	R.M.H.BINNY	C† GARNER	ROBERTS	2	7	130	·	·	8	Spooned simple catch to mid-wicket.	36
2.00	2.30	30	9	MADAN LAL	BOWLED	MARSHALL	17	9	161	1	·	27	Off stump - late on steer stroke.	45
2.19	3.13	54	10	S.M.H.KIRMANI†	BOWLED	HOLDING	14	10	183	·	·	43	Played on via pads.	55
2.32	(3.13)	41	11	B.S.SANDHU	NOT OUT		11			·	1	30		

*CAPTAIN †WICKET-KEEPER EXTRAS b 5 lb 5 w 9 nb 1 = 20 3 6s 15 4s 329 balls (inc 1 no ball)

TOTAL (54.4 OVERS, 227 MIN.) **183** all out at 3.13pm

14 OVERS 3 BALLS/HOUR
3.35 RUNS/OVER
55 RUNS/100 BALLS

BOWLER	O	M	R	W
ROBERTS	10	3	32	3
GARNER	12	4	24	1
MARSHALL	11	1	24	2
HOLDING	9.4	2	26	2
GOMES	11	1	49	2
RICHARDS	1	0	8	0
			20	
	54.4	11	183	10

HRS	OVERS	RUNS		RUNS	MINS	OVERS	LAST 50 (in mins)
1	15	43		50	73	17.3	73
2	14	46		100	134	31.5	61
3	14	66		150	167	40.4	33

LUNCH: 100-4 (32 OVERS) RATE: 3.13 135 MIN.
PATIL 3* (10 min); KAPIL 6* (5 min)

WEST INDIES REQUIRE 184 @ 3.07/OVER

WKT	PARTNERSHIP		RUNS	MINS
1st	Gavaskar	Srikkanth	2	13
2nd	Srikkanth	Amarnath	57	66
3rd	Amarnath	Yashpal	31	40
4th	Yashpal	Patil	2	3
5th	Patil	Kapil	18	8
6th	Patil	Azad	1	1
7th	Patil	Binny	19	9
8th	Patil	Madan	23	17
9th	Madan	Kirmani	8	11
10th	Kirmani	Sandhu	22	41
			183	

compiled by BILL FRINDALL

WEST INDIES INNINGS — REQUIRING 184 TO WIN @ 3.07 PER OVER

IN	OUT	MINS	No.	BATSMAN	HOW OUT	BOWLER	RUNS	WKT	TOTAL	6s	4s	BALLS	NOTES ON DISMISSAL	OVER OUT
3.26	3.37	11	1	C.G.GREENIDGE	BOWLED	SANDHU	1	1	5	·	·	12	No stroke - bowled off pads.	4
3.26	4.10	44	2	D.L.HAYNES	C† BINNY	MADAN LAL	13	2	50	·	2	33	Mistimed drive - cover.	12
3.39	4.20	41	3	I.V.A.RICHARDS	C† KAPIL DEV	MADAN LAL	33	3	57	·	7	28	Hooked skier to mid-wicket (backward running catch).	14
4.12	4.44	32	4	C.H.LLOYD*	C† KAPIL DEV	BINNY	8	5	66	·	1	17	[Restrained groin hitting first ball - Haynes as runner when 1 not out] Mistimed off-drive - mid-off catch.	19
4.22	4.40	18	5	H.A.GOMES	C† GAVASKAR	MADAN LAL	5	4	66	·	·	16	Top-edged cut at short ball.	18
4.42	5.36	34	6	S.F.A.F.BACCHUS	C† KIRMANI	SANDHU	8	6	76	·	·	25	Edged outswinger (widish ball) low in front of slip.	26
4.46	6.39	93	7	P.J.DUJON†	BOWLED	AMARNATH	25	7	119	1	·	73	Changed mind in removing bat - played on.	42
5.38	6.51	73	8	M.D.MARSHALL	C† GAVASKAR	AMARNATH	18	8	124	·	·	51	Flashed at widish ball - edged to slip.	44
6.41	6.56	15	9	A.M.E.ROBERTS	LBW	KAPIL DEV	4	9	126	·	·	14	Played across line.	45
6.52	(7.24)	32	10	J.GARNER	NOT OUT		5			·	·	19		
6.58	7.24	26	11	M.A.HOLDING	LBW	AMARNATH	6	10	140	·	·	24	Ball kept low - played back.	52

*CAPTAIN †WICKET-KEEPER EXTRAS b - lb 4 w 10 nb - = 14 1 6s 10 4s 312 balls (no no-balls)

TOTAL (52 OVERS, 218 MIN) **140** all out at 7.24pm
(WEST INDIES LOWEST PRUDENTIAL CUP TOTAL)

14 OVERS 2 BALLS/HOUR
2.69 RUNS/OVER
45 RUNS/100 BALLS

BOWLER	O	M	R	W
KAPIL DEV	11	4	21	1
SANDHU	9	1	32	2
MADAN LAL	12	2	31	3
BINNY	10	1	23	1
AMARNATH	7	0	12	3
AZAD	3	0	7	0
			14	
	52	8	140	10

HRS	OVERS	RUNS		RUNS	MINS	OVERS	LAST 50
1	14	61		50	44	11.2	44
2	13	19		100	144	33.3	100
3	16	43					

TEA: 76-5 (25 OVERS) RATE: 3.04 108 MIN.
BACCHUS 8* (32 min); DUJON 2* (28 min)
REQUIRING A FURTHER 108 RUNS @ 3.09/OVER

INDIA beat WEST INDIES by **43 runs**
to win 3RD PRUDENTIAL CUP FINAL

MAN OF THE MATCH: M.AMARNATH
(Adjudicator: J.M.Brearley)

WKT	PARTNERSHIP		RUNS	MINS
1st	Greenidge	Haynes	5	11
2nd	Haynes	Richards	45	31
3rd	Richards	Lloyd	7	8
4th	Lloyd	Gomes	9	18
5th	Lloyd	Bacchus	0	2
6th	Bacchus	Dujon	10	30
7th	Dujon	Marshall	43	61
8th	Marshall	Roberts	5	10
9th	Roberts	Garner	2	4
10th	Garner	Holding	14	26
			140	

compiled by BILL FRINDALL